Beyond Firewalls:
Security at scale

By

Naveen Kumar Garg

Beyond Firewalls:
Security at scale

By
Naveen Kumar Garg

Beyond Firewalls: *Security at scale*

First Edition 2024

Copyright © 2024 by Naveen Kumar Garg

All rights reserved, including the right to reproduce this book or portions thereof in any form whatsoever.

ISBN 979-8-9884190-9-9

E-mail : naveenkgrg@gmail.com

Dedicated to my mother

ANITA GARG

(1962–2020)

whose love and support shaped every step of my journey. Her presence gave me strength, and her memory continues to inspire me to reach new heights. Though she is no longer here, her spirit guides me always.

Vision

This book highlights the need for advanced, scalable, and reliable security tools. The author's vision is to merge cybersecurity and system reliability, ensuring security measures can handle peak traffic and evolving threats without fail.

About the Author

Naveen Garg is driven by a deep passion for security and system reliability, combining expertise in Threat Intelligence, Data Analysis, and optimizing complex infrastructures. With years of experience across leading organizations, he has focused on enhancing the scalability and resilience of critical cybersecurity tools. His work emphasizes the importance of creating systems that not only detect threats but also withstand the demands of modern traffic surges and sophisticated attacks. Naveen's commitment to continuous learning and innovation fuels his mission to lead advancements in security solutions that are both efficient and future-ready.

Acknowledgments

I would like to express my deepest appreciation to Krishna Geeni, VP at Akamai, for his groundbreaking vision and leadership in security engineering. Krishna's ability to merge technical excellence with a clear focus on system scalability and reliability has elevated our security platforms to new heights. His dedication to creating high-performance systems with seamless data availability has been a constant source of inspiration, driving innovation and setting the gold standard for security solutions.

I also want to acknowledge Adinarayana Gudla, Director at Akamai, whose remarkable expertise in technology and problem-solving has had an immense impact on my work. Adi's ability to transform complex engineering challenges into innovative solutions, coupled with his unwavering guidance, has shaped my journey toward delivering advanced, high-impact security tools. His mentorship has been pivotal in navigating and achieving critical milestones throughout my career.

Table of Contents

	Vision	4
	About the Author	5
	Acknowledgments	6
	Introduction	9
1.	Cyber Attacks and Traditional Security	13
2.	Beyond Firewalls: The Rise of Modern Cyber Threats	40
3.	Cybersecurity Redefined: Beyond Traditional Defenses	60
4.	Scaling Security: Building Reliable Threat Detection Systems	101
5.	Data at the Core: Ensuring Availability, Localization, and Security	131
6.	AI in Cybersecurity: Balancing Power and Vulnerabilities	144
7.	A Step-by-Step Guide to Building a Robust Security Framework	158

Introduction

Evolving Cybersecurity Landscape

Digital technology has transformed our world. What started with simple programs for basic tasks has now evolved into a complex digital environment. Along with this growth, cyber threats have become more sophisticated, requiring stronger defenses.

In the early days, cybersecurity was straightforward. Simple tools like firewalls and antivirus software were enough to protect against basic threats. But as technology advanced, so did the methods of attackers. The rise of the internet, cloud computing, and connected devices introduced new vulnerabilities. We now face organized and complex attacks like DDoS, ransomware, and advanced persistent threats (APTs).

The introduction of AI has made these attacks even more dangerous. AI-driven attacks can adapt and learn from defenses, making them harder to stop. This shift in the threat landscape demands more advanced cybersecurity tools that can keep up with these challenges.

This book explores how cyber attacks have evolved and how our defenses must evolve too. We'll examine traditional security methods and how to build modern tools that can protect against today's threats. You'll learn how to create advanced cybersecurity solutions that can prevent fraud, protect data, and scale to meet the needs of a connected world.

Why "Beyond Firewalls"?

Traditional cybersecurity focused on securing networks and patching application vulnerabilities, where attackers would typically exploit gaps like open network ports, application flaws, or human errors. For a long time, securing the network, encrypting data, and thoroughly testing applications were considered sufficient to protect against threats. But the landscape has evolved dramatically.

"Today's cyber attackers are no longer limited to exploiting open ports or outdated systems. They employ advanced techniques such as Advanced Persistent Threats (APTs) and Distributed Denial of Service (DDoS) attacks, leveraging cutting-edge technologies like AI and big data to outmaneuver traditional defenses. The challenge has evolved, and attackers are now weaponizing defenders' tools. In this new landscape, relying solely on conventional security measures is no longer sufficient to protect businesses from the sophisticated and relentless threats they face."

This calls for what we term "Beyond Firewalls" Modern cybersecurity must go beyond the basics, capable of distinguishing between legitimate and malicious traffic, and detecting fraudulent activities in real time. The impact of a failure in this defense can be catastrophic. A single DDoS attack can take down critical business applications, and undetected fraudulent transactions can inflict significant financial damage and erode trust.

In the current digital landscape, outdated tools are no match for the advanced, AI-driven attacks that operate at a scale and speed beyond human capabilities. These attacks target everything from personal data to critical infrastructure, often bypassing traditional defenses with ease.

To counter these threats, cybersecurity tools must evolve to become more reliable and adaptive. This book will guide we through the development of advanced cybersecurity tools that not only predict and detect threats but also respond in real time. We will explore how to scale these tools to handle vast amounts of data and traffic, and discuss the critical importance of protecting AI models from being compromised. As AI becomes increasingly central in our digital lives,

Beyond Firewalls: *Security at Scale*

securing it will be paramount to maintaining a reliable and robust cybersecurity posture.

Security at Scale

In the rapidly evolving digital landscape, the scalability, reliability, and availability of security systems are critical to delivering effective protection against advanced threats. Security availability goes beyond merely keeping systems online; it involves ensuring that critical systems are resilient, accessible, and capable of swift recovery in the event of disruptions.

This book explores essential strategies for maintaining security availability, including disaster recovery planning to minimize downtime during unexpected incidents and robust data protection mechanisms that safeguard sensitive information from loss or attacks. We also emphasize the importance of data localization, ensuring that data is stored within specific geographic boundaries to comply with legal and regulatory requirements while remaining protected and accessible.

Scalability is another key focus, as security systems must handle increasing data complexity, traffic surges, and resource demands without compromising performance. We delve into the concepts of redundancy, failover strategies, and the core principles of scalability, guiding we to build security tools that can efficiently manage high traffic, improve response times, and maintain data security under pressure. A security tool that is both scalable and reliable ensures continuous protection, even during peak traffic or sophisticated cyberattacks, without compromising user experience.

Safeguarding AI Models

While AI technology is advancing the sophistication of cyber attacks, it is also vulnerable to being targeted itself. Attackers can poison AI data models, leading to incorrect predictions, or steal the intellectual property of AI models developed by companies. This makes it crucial for AI companies to adopt advanced cybersecurity and data protection measures to keep their AI products safe from attacks.

As AI continues to revolutionize various industries, it has become a prime target for cybercriminals. If AI models are compromised, the consequences can be severe. In finance, for example, a poisoned AI model could approve fraudulent transactions, while in healthcare, it could result in misdiagnoses or incorrect treatment plans.

This book will highlight the importance of protecting AI models from such attacks. We will discuss best practices for securing these models, including techniques to detect and mitigate poisoning attempts. By understanding the unique challenges that AI presents, we can build more resilient systems that safeguard not just the data, but the integrity of the AI models themselves.

Why Now?

The world is rapidly transforming into a digital landscape where individuals' personal data, businesses' financial records, and even the global economy are all intertwined online. Governments, individuals, and businesses alike recognize the critical need for data protection and the importance of blocking fraudulent activities. In today's environment, no business can thrive without robust security measures. However, traditional security approaches are no longer sufficient to combat modern fraud and cyber threats. To keep businesses operational and avoid the severe penalties associated with data breaches and fraud, the evolution to Scalable Cyber Defense is not just necessary—it's urgent.

Traditional security measures are no longer sufficient in the face of modern threats. As we enter the era of highly sophisticated attacks and large-scale traffic surges, we need advanced, adaptable tools to protect both our data and AI models. This book will guide we in developing scalable, resilient cybersecurity solutions to meet the challenges of today's digital landscape and beyond.

Beyond Firewalls: *Security at Scale*

1

Cyber Attacks and Traditional Security

Understanding Cyber Attackers

Before diving into the strategies of cybersecurity, it's crucial to understand the mindset and motives of those we are defending against. Knowing who the attackers are and what drives them provides valuable perspective on the threats we face in the digital space. In this section, we will explore the different categories of cyber attackers, offering insight into their tactics, goals, and the challenges they present.Cyber attackers come in various forms, each driven by different motivations. Some are career cybercriminals seeking financial gain through activities like ransomware or data theft. Others, known as hacktivists, are motivated by political or social causes, aiming to disrupt or embarrass organizations to make a statement.Understanding these diverse motivations is crucial for developing effective cybersecurity strategies to protect against a wide range of threats.

Let's explore the various types of cyber attackers and what drives them:

Career Cybercriminals: In 2017, the WannaCry ransomware attack affected hundreds of thousands of computers across 150 countries. The attackers demanded ransom payments in Bitcoin in exchange for decrypting the infected files. The attack caused significant financial losses and disrupted critical services, including hospitals in the UK.

Hacktivists: The hacker group Anonymous has carried out numerous cyberattacks in the name of social and political causes. For example, in 2010, they launched Operation Payback, targeting organizations like PayPal, Mastercard, and Visa for their refusal to process payments to WikiLeaks, in defense of free speech and transparency.

State-Sponsored Actors: The 2016 cyber attack on the Democratic National Committee (DNC) during the U.S. Presidential election is widely believed to have been conducted by Russian state-sponsored hackers. The breach led to the release of sensitive emails, influencing public opinion and raising concerns about foreign interference in the election process.

Beyond Firewalls: *Security at Scale*

Insiders: In 2013, Edward Snowden, a contractor for the National Security Agency (NSA), leaked classified information about global surveillance programs. His actions exposed extensive government monitoring activities, leading to a global debate on privacy and security.

Thrill-Seekers and Script Kiddies: In 2000, a 15-year-old hacker known as "Mafiaboy" launched a series of distributed denial-of-service (DDoS) attacks that brought down major websites like Yahoo!, eBay, and CNN. The attacks were motivated by the thrill of proving his capabilities rather than financial or ideological reasons.

Organized Crime Groups: The Carbanak cybercrime group, which operated from 2013 to 2018, is responsible for stealing over $1 billion from banks worldwide. They used sophisticated techniques, including spear-phishing and malware, to gain access to internal banking systems and transfer funds to their own accounts.

Terrorist Groups: In 2015, the Islamic State of Iraq and Syria (ISIS) launched a cyberattack on the U.S. Central Command's Twitter and YouTube accounts, posting propaganda messages and threats. Although the attack was more of a psychological operation, it highlighted the potential for cyberterrorism to cause fear and disrupt communication channels.

Impacts of Cyber Attacks:

Cyber attacks can have severe consequences for both businesses and individuals. Businesses may face significant financial losses, reputational damage, and legal issues. Recovery costs, disrupted operations, and lost customer trust can lead to further financial decline. For individuals, the impact often includes financial loss, emotional distress, and damaged personal relationships, along with a lasting psychological toll that erodes trust in digital platforms and creates anxiety about future online interactions.

Impact on Businesses:

Financial Losses: Cyber attacks often result in substantial financial costs, including expenses for repairing compromised systems, paying legal fees, and dealing with lost business opportunities. The financial toll can be further compounded by ransom payments or the loss of intellectual property.

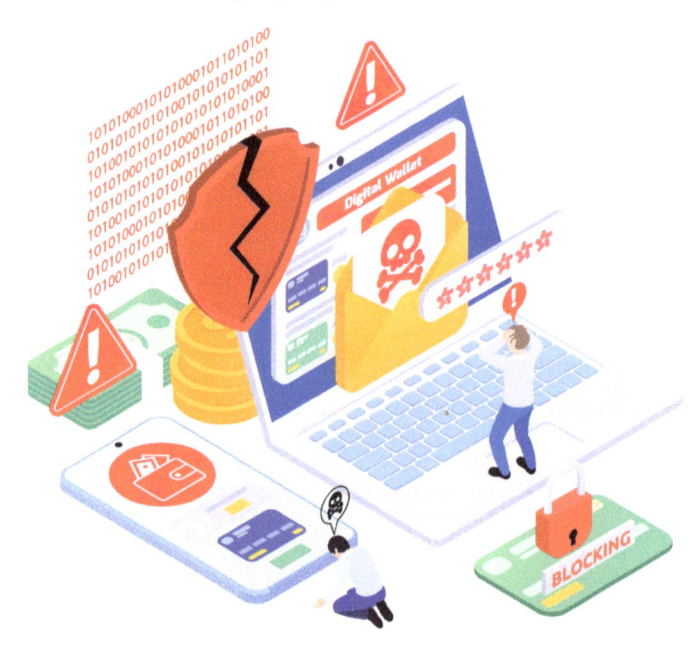

Reputational Damage: A security breach can severely damage a company's reputation. Customers may lose trust in the business, leading to a decline in sales and a tarnished brand image. Rebuilding this trust can take years and may never fully recover.

Operational Disruption: Attacks like Distributed Denial of Service (DDoS) or malware infections can bring business operations to a standstill. The resulting downtime not only affects productivity but can also lead to missed deadlines and lost revenue, especially if critical systems are rendered inoperable.

Legal Consequences: Businesses may face significant legal repercussions if they fail to protect sensitive data. Regulatory bodies can impose fines and sanctions for non-compliance with data protection laws, further adding to the financial burden and complicating recovery efforts.

Customer Attrition: Following a data breach, businesses often experience a loss of customers. Breached data and compromised

Cyber Attacks and Traditional Security

privacy lead to a loss of confidence among consumers, who may choose to take their business elsewhere to avoid potential risks.

Impact on Individuals:

Financial Loss: Individuals can suffer severe financial harm from cyber attacks, including identity theft, unauthorized transactions, and drained bank accounts. Recovering from these losses can be a lengthy and stressful process, often involving legal battles and prolonged financial instability.

Emotional Distress: The violation of personal privacy can lead to significant emotional distress. Victims may experience anxiety, fear, and a pervasive sense of insecurity, knowing that their personal information has been exposed or exploited.

Personal Harm: Cyber attacks can lead to the exposure of sensitive or private information, resulting in long-term emotional distress, such as blackmail or shaming.

Professional Repercussions: Leaked information can cause damage to a person's professional image, impacting career prospects and creating mistrust in business or social networks.

Social Isolation: Public defamation or breach of personal data can harm relationships and lead to social isolation, with friends, family, or colleagues distancing themselves due to the stigma.

Productivity Loss: When individuals are locked out of essential systems due to ransomware or other cyber attacks, their daily activities and professional responsibilities are disrupted. This can lead to missed opportunities, financial setbacks, and long-term consequences in their personal and professional lives.

Psychological Impact: The psychological toll of cyber attacks is profound. Victims often suffer from increased stress, sleep disturbances, and a persistent sense of vulnerability. The ongoing threat of cybercrime can create a state of constant unease, affecting overall well-being and mental health.

Trust Erosion: Repeated exposure to cyber threats can erode an individual's trust in digital services and technology. This loss of confidence may deter them from adopting new technologies or participating in online activities, limiting their ability to benefit fully from the digital world.

Cyber attacks pose serious threats to both businesses and individuals, leading to financial losses, reputational damage, and significant emotional and psychological impacts. The evolving nature of these threats makes it essential for both entities to adopt robust cybersecurity measures to protect their assets, maintain trust, and ensure long-term stability in an increasingly digital world.

Core Principles of Traditional Cybersecurity

In the increasingly complex landscape of digital threats, understanding the key categories of cybersecurity and the principles that underpin them is essential for building robust defenses. Each category addresses specific aspects of security and is designed to counter different types of cyberattacks. This chapter outlines the fundamental cybersecurity categories, the types of attacks they combat, and the principles that guide effective security strategies.

Network security

Network security is the practice of safeguarding computer networks from unauthorized access, misuse, or attacks. This involves implementing multiple layers of defense to ensure the network remains secure, operational, and resilient against cyber threats. Effective network security allows authorized users to access resources while blocking malicious actors, thus protecting sensitive data, maintaining reliable performance, and safeguarding a company's reputation.

Cyber Attacks Countered by Network Security

Distributed Denial of Service (DDoS): A DDoS attack overwhelms a network, server, or website with excessive traffic, rendering services unavailable to legitimate users.

Example: In 2016, the Dyn DNS provider was hit by a massive DDoS attack that disrupted major websites like Twitter, Netflix, and Reddit for several hours.

Man-in-the-Middle (MitM) Attacks: In a MitM attack, the attacker secretly intercepts and alters communication between two parties. This can occur on unsecured Wi-Fi networks, where attackers can eavesdrop on data being transmitted.

Example: An attacker might intercept the communication between a user and their bank, altering the data to siphon off funds or steal login credentials.

Network Intrusion: Network intrusion occurs when an attacker gains unauthorized access to a network, often using malware or exploiting vulnerabilities.

Example: The 2013 Target breach, where hackers infiltrated the retailer's network through a third-party vendor, eventually gaining access to the payment system and compromising millions of customers' credit card information.

Ransomware Attacks: Ransomware encrypts the victim's data, rendering it inaccessible until a ransom is paid for the decryption key.

Example: The WannaCry ransomware attack in 2017 affected hundreds of thousands of computers worldwide, including critical infrastructure like hospitals, demanding payment in Bitcoin for the release of the encrypted data.

Key Components of Network Security

Firewalls: A firewall acts as a barrier between trusted internal networks and untrusted external networks. It monitors, filters, and controls incoming and outgoing traffic based on predefined security rules. Firewalls have evolved significantly, from basic packet filtering to Next-Generation Firewalls (NGFWs) that inspect data packets deeply and block sophisticated threats like malware and application-layer attacks.

Example: In 2003, the SQL Slammer worm spread rapidly by exploiting a vulnerability in Microsoft SQL Server. Networks with properly configured firewalls were able to block the worm, preventing widespread damage.

Intrusion Prevention Systems (IPS): An IPS detects and blocks known and suspected threats before they can impact the network core or edge devices. It performs deep packet inspection, including inspection of encrypted traffic, and can provide virtual patching to mitigate vulnerabilities at the network level.

Example: In 2013, IPS systems played a crucial role in identifying the Target data breach. Although the breach resulted in significant data loss, the IPS alerts helped in the eventual containment of the attack.

Network Segmentation: Network segmentation involves dividing a network into smaller, isolated segments, each with its own security controls. This helps contain potential breaches by limiting access to specific areas of the network.

Example: During the WannaCry ransomware attack in 2017, organizations with network segmentation were able to limit the spread of the malware, reducing its overall impact.

Access Control: Access control ensures that only authorized users and devices can interact with sensitive resources. This can be enforced through Role-Based Access Control (RBAC) and Identity and Access Management (IAM) systems.

Example: In 2020, Twitter suffered a high-profile breach when attackers exploited weak access controls, gaining access to internal tools and compromising numerous high-profile accounts. This incident highlighted the importance of strict access control measures.

Remote Access VPNs: Remote Access VPNs provide secure connections for remote users to access corporate networks. They create a private, encrypted connection from a public Wi-Fi network, ensuring that data remains secure during transmission.

Example: During the COVID-19 pandemic, the surge in remote work made VPNs critical for maintaining secure access to corporate resources.

Encryption: Encryption transforms readable data into a coded format, making it unreadable to unauthorized parties. It is vital for protecting sensitive information, especially when transmitted over the internet.

Example: In 2016, the FBI's request for Apple to unlock an encrypted iPhone brought encryption into the spotlight, emphasizing its importance in protecting user data from unauthorized access.

Data Loss Prevention (DLP): DLP solutions help prevent sensitive information from being shared outside of the organization, whether accidentally or maliciously. This is especially important for protecting regulated data like personally identifiable information (PII) and compliance-related data.

Zero Trust Network Access (ZTNA): ZTNA operates on the principle of "never trust, always verify," ensuring that users only have access to the resources they need to perform their duties. Unlike traditional security solutions, ZTNA enforces granular access controls, improving overall security.

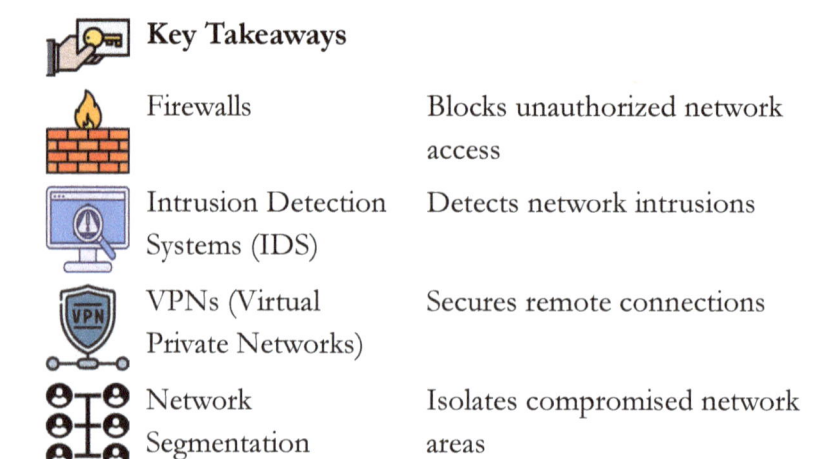

Key Takeaways

	Firewalls	Blocks unauthorized network access
	Intrusion Detection Systems (IDS)	Detects network intrusions
	VPNs (Virtual Private Networks)	Secures remote connections
	Network Segmentation	Isolates compromised network areas

Application Security

Application security is crucial for protecting software from unauthorized access and cyber threats throughout its lifecycle, from design to deployment and beyond. As applications become more connected, especially with the rise of cloud computing, they face increased vulnerability to attacks. Hackers now target applications directly, exploiting weaknesses to access sensitive data or disrupt services. For example, SQL injection attacks can breach application databases, leading to significant data losses. Embedding security into every stage of development is essential to prevent such attacks and safeguard both the application and its data. Applications can be broadly categorized into three categories as follows

Web Applications: High-profile targets like Amazon or PayPal are vulnerable due to their internet exposure. For instance, the 2017 Equifax breach, stemming from a web app vulnerability, compromised millions of personal records. Protecting against threats like SQL injection and XSS is essential.

APIs: APIs, such as those used by Twitter and Facebook, connect various systems but are vulnerable if insecure. The 2018 Facebook breach, caused by API flaws, exposed millions of user accounts, highlighting the need for strong authentication and encryption.

Cloud-Native Applications: Cloud-native apps like Netflix, which rely on microservices and containers, offer scalability but also complexity. A compromised container can threaten the entire system, necessitating specialized security tools like Infrastructure as Code (IaC) and continuous monitoring.

Application Vulenrabilites Attacks

Application security focuses on protecting software applications from various types of cyberattacks. Here are some of the key attacks covered under application security:

SQL Injection: Attackers inject malicious SQL code into a web application's database query, allowing them to access, modify, or delete data. For example, by entering SQL code into a login form, an attacker might bypass authentication and gain unauthorized access.

Cross-Site Scripting (XSS): Malicious scripts are injected into web pages viewed by other users, potentially stealing session cookies or redirecting users to harmful sites. An example is an attacker injecting a script into a blog's comment section, which then compromises viewers' accounts.

Cross-Site Request Forgery (CSRF): Attackers trick users into executing unwanted actions on a web application where they are authenticated, like transferring funds. For instance, an attacker sends a link that, when clicked by a logged-in user, triggers a money transfer to the attacker's account.

Remote Code Execution (RCE): This vulnerability allows attackers to execute arbitrary code on a server or client machine. An attacker could exploit a web application's file upload feature to upload and run malicious code on the server.

Buffer Overflow: Attackers exploit a program's memory buffer to overwrite adjacent memory locations, potentially leading to code execution. For example, an application might crash or run malicious code if an attacker inputs more data than the buffer can handle.

Insecure Deserialization: Attackers exploit flaws in deserializing data to execute code, modify data, or perform attacks. For instance, an attacker sends a malicious serialized object that, when deserialized by the application, triggers harmful actions on the server.

Zero-Day Exploits: These attacks target unknown vulnerabilities in an application before developers can patch them. An example is an attacker exploiting a security flaw in a newly released feature that developers have not yet identified.

Session Hijacking: Attackers steal or manipulate a user's session ID to impersonate them and gain unauthorized access. For example, an attacker intercepts a session ID over an unsecured network and uses it to log in as the legitimate user.

Directory Traversal: Attackers manipulate URLs or input fields to access directories and files outside the web root. For instance, by entering "../" in a URL, an attacker could access sensitive files like configuration files or passwords.

Security Misconfiguration: This occurs when settings are improperly configured or default configurations are left unchanged, making applications vulnerable. An example is an application with debug mode enabled in production, which might expose sensitive information or allow unauthorized access.

Key Components of Application Security

Authentication: Authentication is the first line of defense in application security. It ensures that only authorized users can access the application. This process can be as simple as requiring a username and password, but more secure methods like multi-factor authentication (MFA) are increasingly common. MFA adds layers to the authentication process, such as requiring a code sent to a user's mobile device or biometric verification like fingerprint scanning.

Authorization: After authentication, authorization determines what an authenticated user can access within the application. It acts as a gatekeeper, ensuring that users can only access the resources they are permitted to use. For example, in a financial application, an employee might be authenticated to log in but only authorized to view certain account information, not all financial data.

Encryption: Encryption is vital for protecting sensitive data within an application. It converts data into a secure format that unauthorized users cannot read. For example, in cloud-based applications, encryption ensures that data traveling between the user and the cloud remains secure, even if intercepted by cybercriminals.

Logging: Logging provides a trail of evidence in case of a security breach. It records who accessed the application, when, and what actions were taken. This information is crucial for identifying how an attack occurred and mitigating future risks. For instance, if an unauthorized user accessed sensitive data, the logs can help trace the breach's origin and impact.

Application Security Testing: Regular testing is essential to ensure that all security measures are functioning correctly. Application security testing can identify vulnerabilities before attackers exploit them. Techniques like penetration testing simulate attacks to assess the application's defenses, helping developers fix potential weaknesses.

Key Takeaways

Technique	Major Cyber Attacks Handled
Code Reviews	Identifies and fixes vulnerabilities
Application Firewalls	Blocks malicious application traffic

Penetration Testing	Uncovers application security flaws
Patch Management	Fixes known vulnerabilities
Input Validation	Prevents SQL injections and XSS attacks

Information Security

Information security (InfoSec) is the practice of protecting information, both digital and physical, from unauthorized access, misuse, disclosure, disruption, or destruction. As organizations increasingly rely on digital data and interconnected systems, InfoSec has become a critical component in safeguarding sensitive information, ensuring business continuity, and maintaining trust with clients and stakeholders. The primary goal of InfoSec is to protect the confidentiality, integrity, and availability of data, often referred to as the CIA Triad.

Top Information Security Threats

Organizations face a variety of threats that can compromise their information security:

Phishing: Attackers use deceptive emails or messages to trick individuals into revealing sensitive information, such as login credentials or financial details. Phishing remains one of the most common and effective attack methods.

Malware: Malicious software, such as viruses, worms, and ransomware, is designed to damage, disrupt, or gain unauthorized access to systems. Malware can spread through email attachments, infected websites, or compromised software.

Insider Threats: Employees or other trusted individuals may intentionally or accidentally cause security breaches by mishandling data or granting unauthorized access. Insider threats can be challenging to detect and prevent.

Social Engineering: Attackers manipulate individuals into performing actions or divulging confidential information by exploiting psychological triggers like trust, fear, or urgency. Social engineering attacks often bypass technical defenses.

Data Breaches: Unauthorized access to confidential data, often resulting in its theft, exposure, or manipulation. Data breaches can lead to financial loss, reputational damage, and legal consequences.

Principles of Information Security

InfoSec is built on three fundamental principles:

Confidentiality: Ensures that information is accessible only to those with authorized access. This is achieved through encryption, access control, and secure authentication methods. Protecting confidentiality helps prevent sensitive data from falling into the wrong hands.

Integrity: Ensures that information remains accurate, complete, and unaltered during storage, processing, and transmission. Integrity is maintained through the use of checksums, digital signatures, and version control systems. This principle protects against unauthorized data modification, ensuring that the information remains trustworthy.

Availability: Ensures that information and resources are available to authorized users when needed. Availability is supported by robust backup systems, redundancy, and disaster recovery plans. This principle is vital for maintaining the functionality of systems and ensuring continuous access to data.

Common Information Security Frameworks

To manage and enhance information security practices, organizations often adopt standardized frameworks:

ISO/IEC 27001: An international standard that provides a systematic approach to managing sensitive information, focusing on implementing and continually improving an Information Security Management System (ISMS).

NIST Cybersecurity Framework: Developed by the National Institute of Standards and Technology (NIST), this framework provides guidelines for organizations to manage and reduce cybersecurity risks. It includes best practices for identifying, protecting, detecting, responding to, and recovering from cyber threats.

COBIT (Control Objectives for Information and Related Technologies): A framework for IT management and governance that helps organizations align their IT goals with business objectives, including information security.

GDPR (General Data Protection Regulation): A European Union regulation that governs data protection and privacy. GDPR imposes strict requirements on how organizations handle personal data and mandates significant penalties for non-compliance.

Steps to Achieve Information Security

Identify and Classify Information Assets: Begin by identifying all information assets within the organization, including databases, intellectual property, and customer data. Classify these assets based on their sensitivity and importance to prioritize security efforts and allocate resources effectively.

Implement Access Controls: Restrict access to sensitive information following the principle of least privilege. Utilize multi-factor authentication (MFA), role-based access control (RBAC), and identity and access management (IAM) systems to limit access, reducing the risk of unauthorized entry and potential data breaches.

Ensure Data Confidentiality: Protect data confidentiality by encrypting data both at rest and in transit using secure protocols like SSL/TLS and encryption standards such as AES. This ensures that even if intercepted, the data remains unreadable and secure.

Maintain Data Integrity: Use checksums, cryptographic hash functions, and digital signatures to verify data integrity during storage and transmission. Implement version control systems to track changes and prevent unauthorized modifications, ensuring data remains accurate and trustworthy.

Ensure Data Availability: Implement robust backup solutions and redundancy measures to guarantee data availability. Regularly test disaster recovery plans to minimize downtime during cyberattacks, hardware failures, or natural disasters, ensuring uninterrupted access for authorized users.

Develop and Enforce Security Policies: Establish comprehensive security policies covering data handling, access control, and incident response. Regularly review, update, and communicate these policies to ensure consistent and secure information management across the organization.

Regular Security Audits and Monitoring: Conduct regular security audits to identify vulnerabilities and ensure compliance with policies. Implement continuous monitoring tools to detect suspicious activities in real time, proactively addressing security gaps before they are exploited.

Implement Incident ResponsePlans: Develop an incident response plan outlining procedures for identifying, containing, and mitigating security breaches. Include clear communication channels and roles for stakeholders to enable quick reaction, minimizing damage and restoring normal operations swiftly.

Information security relies on the principles of confidentiality, integrity, and availability. By identifying critical assets, enforcing strong access controls, and utilizing technologies like encryption and DLP, organizations can protect data from unauthorized access while ensuring its accuracy and availability. Regular audits, continuous improvement, and employee training enhance the security framework, safeguarding against evolving threats and ensuring resilience. Adhering to these practices also helps organizations mitigate risks and comply with legal and regulatory requirements.

Key Takeaways

	Encryption	Protects data confidentiality
	Access Control	Limits data access to authorized users
	Data Loss Prevention (DLP)	Prevents sensitive data leaks
	Backup and Recovery	Mitigates data loss from ransomware
	Audit Trails	Tracks unauthorized data access

Operational Security

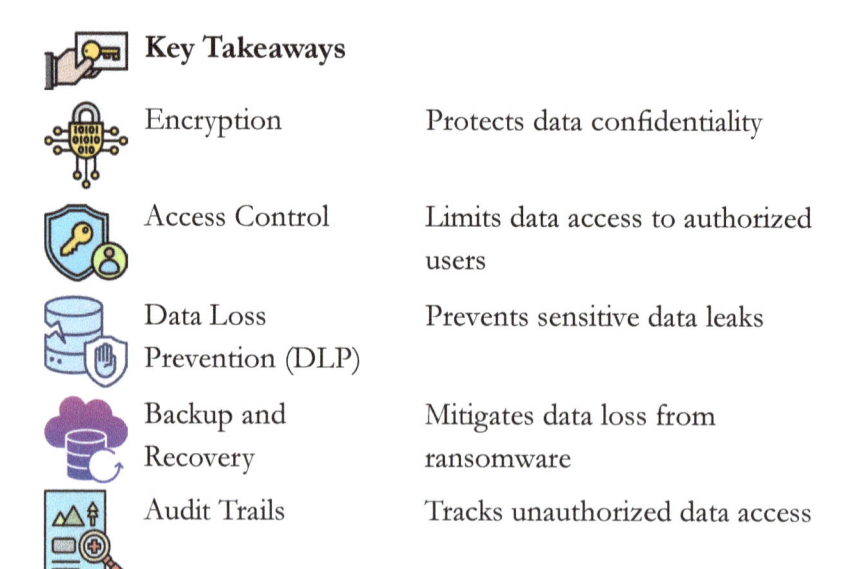

Operational Security (OPSEC) is a comprehensive strategy designed to safeguard sensitive information from falling into the wrong hands. It's about staying one step ahead of potential attackers by predicting their methods and closing any gaps they might exploit. Essentially, OPSEC encourages organizations to view their operations from the perspective of a potential hacker, identifying and mitigating vulnerabilities before they can be exploited. This proactive approach is crucial in ensuring that both physical and digital assets remain secure and that sensitive information is protected.

Top Operation Security Threats:

Operational Security (OPSEC) is designed to mitigate several critical risks that organizations face in today's digital landscape:

Beyond Firewalls: *Security at Scale*

Unauthorized Access: Protects sensitive data and systems from unauthorized individuals, ensuring that only those with proper credentials can access crucial information.

Insider Threats: Mitigates risks posed by internal personnel who may misuse their access, safeguarding against potential sabotage or data leaks.

Data Breaches: Prevents the exposure of confidential information to external attackers, maintaining the integrity and trustworthiness of the organization.

Operational Disruptions: Minimizes the impact of cyberattacks or other security incidents on business operations through effective incident response and disaster recovery planning.

Intellectual Property Theft: Protects valuable company innovations and trade secrets, ensuring that the organization maintains its competitive edge.

How Operational Security Works

Here's the same write-up with shorter titles:

Identifying Critical Assets: Operational Security (OPSEC) begins with identifying the organization's most valuable assets that require protection. This could include intellectual property, financial data, customer information, or operational procedures. By pinpointing what is most valuable, organizations can focus their security efforts effectively. For instance, a technology company might prioritize securing its research and development data, recognizing it as a prime target for competitors or hackers.

Anticipating Threats: Once critical assets are identified, the next step is to determine the potential threats that could endanger these assets. Threats can originate from external sources, such as hackers, or internal sources, such as disgruntled employees. Understanding who might exploit vulnerabilities and how they might do so is crucial for developing effective defenses. For example, a financial institution might consider cybercriminals as a significant threat, given their motivation to steal sensitive customer data for financial gain.

Identifying Vulnerabilities: After identifying potential threats, organizations must evaluate their current security measures to identify vulnerabilities that could be exploited. These could include outdated software, gaps in physical security, or insufficient employee training. Recognizing these weaknesses allows organizations to address them before they can be exploited. For instance, a retail company might discover that its payment processing system uses outdated encryption, making it susceptible to cyberattacks.

Assessing risks and Implementing Safeguards: Risk assessment involves evaluating the likelihood of threats exploiting identified vulnerabilities and the potential impact of such events. This process helps prioritize which vulnerabilities require immediate attention. For instance, an e-commerce platform with a vulnerability that could expose thousands of customer credit card numbers would classify this issue as high risk, necessitating prompt action. To mitigate these risks, organizations must implement safeguards such as updating security policies, adopting new technologies, or enhancing employee training. For example, a healthcare provider might strengthen encryption protocols, establish strict access controls, and automate security updates to protect patient data.

Real-World Example and Best Practices: To maintain robust security, organizations must adopt key best practices, including continuous monitoring and auditing of network changes, enforcing access controls based on necessity, applying the principle of least privilege, and automating routine security tasks. Additionally, preparing for worst-case scenarios through comprehensive disaster recovery and business continuity plans is essential. For example, a multinational corporation managing extensive customer data across multiple regions might identify customer data as a critical asset, recognize cybercriminals as primary threats, and pinpoint outdated encryption as a vulnerability. By assessing the risk of a potential data breach as catastrophic, the company can implement advanced encryption, enforce strict access controls, and automate security updates, thereby effectively mitigating risks and safeguarding sensitive information.

In summary, OPSEC is about thinking ahead, anticipating threats, and taking proactive steps to protect critical assets. By integrating a thorough process of identifying assets, assessing threats, addressing vulnerabilities, and continuously monitoring and improving security practices, organizations can maintain a strong security posture in an increasingly complex threat landscape.

Key Takeaways

	Change Management	Prevents unauthorized system changes
	Dual Control	Separates network and security duties

Cyber Attacks and Traditional Security

Automation	Reduces human error in security tasks
Incident Response Plan	Manages security breaches effectively
Access Control and Logging	Monitors and restricts system access

Conclusion:

In this chapter, we explored the evolution of cyber threats and the traditional methods used to counter them. We discussed how the digital landscape has transformed into a complex network vulnerable to sophisticated attacks, revealing the limitations of traditional cybersecurity approaches. These methods, built on principles like confidentiality, integrity, availability, and authentication, are foundational but increasingly insufficient against modern threats driven by AI and large-scale data breaches. While essential, traditional defenses can be bypassed by advanced tactics like phishing, insider threats, and DDoS attacks, highlighting the need for more intelligent and adaptive security measures.

In the next chapter, we will delve into advanced cyber attacks, exploring how they exploit the gaps in traditional defenses and what new strategies are needed to counter them. This will set the stage for developing the next generation of cybersecurity solutions to protect against these evolving threats.

References:

https://www.spiceworks.com/it-security/security-general/articles/what-is-operations-security-opsec/

https://www.securitystudio.com/blog/operational-security

https://www.checkpoint.com/cyber-hub/network-security/what-is-network-security/

https://www.cisco.com/c/en/us/products/security/what-is-network-security.html

https://www.fortinet.com/resources/cyberglossary/what-is-network-security

2

Beyond Firewalls: The Rise of Modern Cyber Threats

Traditional cybersecurity methods refer to the foundational practices that have been used to protect digital assets and networks from threats over the years. These include tools like firewalls, which act as barriers between secure internal networks and external threats, and antivirus software, designed to detect and remove malicious programs. Intrusion Detection Systems (IDS) monitor network traffic for suspicious activity, while security awareness training educates employees on best practices to prevent breaches.

Emerging Challenges in Cybersecurity

Traditional cybersecurity methods, once highly effective against common threats like viruses and unauthorized access, are now being outpaced by the rapid evolution of cyber threats. Firewalls and antivirus programs, which were once the first line of defense, are now often insufficient against the sophisticated attacks emerging today.

The Evolving Threat Landscape: As cyber threats have advanced, so has malware, which now includes complex variants that can bypass traditional antivirus protections. Modern malware takes advantage of the increasing number of internet-connected devices, exploiting vulnerabilities that older security measures cannot address. Proactive, real-time monitoring is now essential to detect and neutralize threats before they cause significant damage.

The Need for Proactive Defense: Traditional security measures are inherently reactive, responding to threats only after they have been detected. In the current cyber landscape, where new threats emerge daily, this approach is no longer viable. By the time traditional defenses activate, the damage may already be done. Organizations must adopt proactive defense strategies that anticipate and prevent attacks before they occur.

Precision Attacks and Social Engineering: Cybercriminals are increasingly employing precision attacks, such as social engineering, that target human vulnerabilities rather than technological ones. These attacks manipulate individuals into compromising security, making them difficult to detect with traditional tools. Raising awareness and implementing robust training programs are critical to defending against these deceptive tactics.

The Expanding Cybercrime Ecosystem: The rise of the Internet of Things (IoT) has introduced countless new devices into the digital ecosystem, each a potential entry point for attackers. Cybercriminals now target entire systems or supply chains, requiring dynamic and adaptable cybersecurity strategies that evolve alongside these emerging threats.

Inadequate Crisis Training: Many organizations still rely on outdated crisis training that does not reflect the complexity of modern cyber threats. These training programs often lack realism and fail to prepare employees for the sophisticated nature of current attacks. Effective crisis training should simulate real-world scenarios, ensuring that organizations are better equipped to respond to actual incidents.

Insider Threats and Internal Vulnerabilities: Traditional security tools focus primarily on external threats, often overlooking the significant risks posed by malicious insiders or compromised accounts. Without proper monitoring of user behavior and access patterns, organizations can miss critical signs of internal breaches, leading to undetected data theft or unauthorized access.

The Burden of False Positives: Security systems that generate a high volume of false positives can overwhelm security teams, leading to alert fatigue. This not only wastes resources but also increases the risk that genuine threats will be overlooked. Reducing false positives is crucial for maintaining the effectiveness of security operations.

Challenges in Adapting to New Technologies: The rapid adoption of technologies like cloud computing, IoT, and mobile environments has exposed the limitations of traditional security measures. These tools struggle to protect cloud-native applications and complex IT environments, leaving organizations vulnerable to new and evolving risks.

The Vulnerability of Remote Work: The shift to remote work has expanded the security perimeter, increasing risks as employees operate outside of secure networks. Traditional security solutions, designed for on-premises environments, are often inadequate for protecting a dispersed workforce from sophisticated threats like phishing and ransomware.

Human Error and Social Engineering: Despite extensive investment in user training, human error remains a critical vulnerability. Social engineering attacks continue to exploit this weakness, proving that relying solely on human vigilance is not enough. Organizations must complement training with technological defenses that do not depend entirely on user behavior.

Modern Cybersecurity attacks:

Today's cyber threats have outpaced traditional security measures, requiring more advanced strategies. Attackers now use sophisticated tools and tactics that demand a proactive defense.

Automation and Exploit Kits: Automation tools and exploit kits have lowered the barrier for launching complex attacks. These tools enable attackers to quickly exploit known vulnerabilities on a large scale, making traditional defenses less effective.

Supply Chain Attacks: Attackers increasingly target supply chains, exploiting trusted vendor relationships to infiltrate larger organizations. The SolarWinds breach exemplifies how a single compromised vendor can lead to widespread damage.

Zero-Day Exploits: Zero-day vulnerabilities pose a significant challenge, as they are unknown to vendors and can be exploited before patches are available. This makes them particularly dangerous, requiring advanced detection methods beyond traditional security.

AI-Powered Attacks: AI and machine learning have transformed cyberattacks, enabling more adaptive and hard-to-detect methods. AI-driven phishing and deepfake technologies create sophisticated threats that traditional defenses struggle to counter.

Multi-Vector Attacks: Attackers now deploy multi-vector attacks, combining methods like phishing and malware to breach systems. These complex assaults require integrated security solutions to defend against coordinated threats.

Recent Examples of Advanced Cyber Threats

Here are some recent examples that illustrate how attackers have become increasingly sophisticated in their methods, deploying complex DDoS attacks that challenge traditional cybersecurity defenses. These incidents highlight the necessity for advanced tools and strategies to effectively mitigate such threats:

GitHub DDoS Attack (2018): In February 2018, GitHub, one of the largest code hosting platforms, faced a record-breaking DDoS attack with a peak of 1.35 Tbps. This attack leveraged the Memcached vulnerability and was mitigated within minutes by Akamai's Prolexic service, which rerouted and absorbed the massive traffic.

Reference: https://www.wired.com/story/github-ddos-memcached/

Dyn DNS Attack (2016): A massive DDoS attack targeted Dyn, a major DNS provider, in October 2016. The attack, which involved a botnet of IoT devices, severely disrupted internet services across the United States, taking down major websites like Twitter, Netflix, and Reddit. The attack highlighted vulnerabilities in IoT security.

Reference: https://krebsonsecurity.com/2016/10/ddos-on-dyn-impacts-twitter-spotify-reddit/

Spamhaus DDoS Attack (2013): In March 2013, Spamhaus, an organization that tracks spam-related activity, was hit by a 300 Gbps DDoS attack, one of the largest at the time. The attack was so large that it reportedly slowed down global internet traffic. The attack was eventually mitigated by Cloudflare.

Reference: https://www.bbc.com/news/technology-21954636

KrebsOnSecurity DDoS Attack (2016): In September 2016, the cybersecurity blog KrebsOnSecurity was taken offline by a 620 Gbps DDoS attack. The attack used a botnet of compromised IoT devices and was one of the largest DDoS attacks at that time. It led to increased awareness of IoT security risks.

Reference: https://krebsonsecurity.com/2016/09/krebsonsecurity-hit-with-record-ddos/

BBC DDoS Attack (2015): The BBC's website was hit by a DDoS attack in December 2015, during the holiday season. The attack peaked at 602 Gbps and caused significant disruption to the BBC's online services. The attack was a stark reminder of the vulnerabilities faced by high-profile media organizations.

Reference: https://www.bbc.com/news/technology-35204915

Key Takeaways

	Advanced Persistent Threats	Stealthy, persistent attacks evading basic defenses.
	Botnet-Driven DDoS Attacks	Massive attacks that flood systems, needing advanced filters
	Sophisticated Social Engineering	Targeted attacks like spear-phishing, deepfakes, need behavioral analysis.
	AI-Powered Cyber Attacks	AI-driven adaptive attacks bypass traditional tools

Beyond Firewalls: The Rise of Modern Cyber Threats

How Technology Boosts Cybercriminal Capabilities

Accessible Cloud Computing: Cloud computing has drastically reduced the barriers to launching cyber attacks. Attackers can now rent computing power by the hour, making it easier and cheaper to conduct large-scale operations like Distributed Denial of Service (DDoS) attacks. For example, what once required significant resources can now be accomplished with minimal investment, allowing even low-budget attackers to generate the computational force necessary to overwhelm targeted systems.

Proliferation of IoT Devices: The explosion of Internet of Things (IoT) devices has created a vast number of poorly secured endpoints that attackers can easily compromise and use in powerful botnets. The Mirai botnet, for instance, exploited vulnerable IoT devices to launch one of the largest DDoS attacks in history, demonstrating how the widespread adoption of IoT has transformed the scale and impact of cyber attacks.

Advanced Data Analytics: With the rise of big data and sophisticated analytical tools, attackers can now craft highly targeted attacks, such as spear-phishing, that are difficult to detect. Unlike the broad, generalized attacks of the past, modern attackers use detailed analysis of personal information, often gathered from social media, to exploit specific vulnerabilities, increasing the likelihood of successful breaches.

Automation and AI in Cyber Attacks: Automation and artificial intelligence (AI) have revolutionized cyber attacks, making them faster, more adaptive, and less dependent on human intervention.

AI-driven attacks can learn from the defenses they encounter and adjust in real-time, making them more persistent and harder to counter. This evolution creates a moving target that traditional defenses struggle to keep up with, underscoring the need for advanced defensive measures.

Open-Source Technology: The availability of open-source tools has democratized the ability to launch sophisticated cyber attacks. In the past, attackers needed to develop their own tools or purchase expensive software. Today, open-source technologies, complete with documentation and community support, allow even less skilled attackers to deploy advanced techniques, such as creating ransomware using open-source cryptographic libraries, lowering the barrier to entry for launching complex attacks.

Key Takeaways

	Exploit Kits	Attackers use pre-built tools for automated, fast, and scalable attacks.
	Supply Chain Attacks	Infiltrations via third-party vendors compromise larger systems.
	Zero-Day Vulnerabilities	Unpatched software is targeted, bypassing traditional defenses.
	AI-Powered Attacks	AI enhances attackers' strategies, making threats more sophisticated and harder to detect

Beyond Firewalls: The Rise of Modern Cyber Threats

	Advanced DDoS Attacks	Botnets amplify traffic, overwhelming targets with massive, distributed attacks.
	User Credential Theft	Phishing and credential stuffing lead to account takeovers.

Complex Cyber Threats: A New Age of Challenges

As cyber threats become more sophisticated, the need for advanced detection mechanisms has grown exponentially. Traditional security measures, which rely heavily on predefined rules and static defenses, are no longer sufficient. Modern cybersecurity strategies employ advanced techniques that focus on behavior analysis, anomaly detection, and fraud identification to combat emerging threats. Here are some key terminologies and concepts that are essential to understanding advanced threat detection:

Good Bots vs. Bad Bots: Understanding Their Impact

Bots are automated software designed to perform repetitive tasks faster than humans. They can be beneficial or harmful, making it essential to distinguish between good and bad bots to maintain a secure online environment.

Good Bots: Good bots enhance internet functionality by performing helpful tasks.

- **Search Engine Bots:** These crawlers, like Googlebot, index web pages, making them searchable and improving online visibility. For example, when a new website launches, search engine bots crawl it to make content available in search results.

Beyond Firewalls: *Security at Scale*

- **Content Aggregation Bots:** These bots gather and organize content from various sources, like news aggregators, ensuring users access the latest information quickly.

- **Monitoring Bots:** These bots track website performance, notifying administrators of issues like downtime, allowing for prompt action to maintain optimal site performance.

Bad Bots: Bad bots are malicious programs that cause harm by engaging in activities like data theft and service disruption.

- **Web Scraping Bots:** These bots steal sensitive information, such as pricing data, from websites, which can then be used fraudulently or sold.

- **Credential Stuffing Bots:** These bots use stolen login credentials to access user accounts, leading to identity theft or financial fraud.

- **DDoS Bots:** These bots flood a website with traffic, causing it to crash and become inaccessible to legitimate users.

- **Ad Fraud Bots:** These bots generate fake clicks on ads, costing advertisers money without generating actual customer engagement.

Botnets: Botnets are networks of compromised devices controlled by a malicious actor. Botnets can launch large-scale attacks, like DDoS, using vast computing power from infected devices. For example, the Mirai botnet disrupted internet services across the U.S. in 2016 by hijacking IoT devices.

Why Differentiating Matters: Understanding the difference between good and bad bots is crucial. Blocking all bots can harm

Beyond Firewalls: The Rise of Modern Cyber Threats

essential functions like search engine indexing, reducing a website's visibility. Conversely, failing to block malicious bots can lead to data breaches, service disruptions, and financial losses.

Intent Behind Bot Attacks

Bot attacks are orchestrated with various malicious intents, ranging from financial gain to data theft, disruption of services, or even corporate espionage. Attackers use bots to automate repetitive tasks at a scale and speed far beyond human capabilities, enabling them to execute massive attacks with minimal effort. The ultimate goal of these attacks varies, but it typically involves:

Stealing sensitive information: such as user credentials or credit card details.

Disrupting services: through Distributed Denial of Service (DDoS) attacks.

Performing automated transactions: for activities like ticket scalping or sniping limited-edition products.

Spamming: Spreading malicious content across platforms.

These bots can overwhelm systems, leading to significant financial losses, reputation damage, and compromised user trust.

How Attackers Conduct Bot Attacks

Attackers use various methods to conduct bot attacks, often combining multiple techniques to increase their success rates. Some of the most common methods include:

Credential Stuffing: Bots use stolen usernames and passwords, often sourced from data breaches, to attempt logins on multiple platforms. Successful logins result in account takeovers and unauthorized transactions.

Web Scraping: Bots extract large amounts of data from websites, such as pricing information, content, or user data, which can then be used for competitive advantage or sold on the dark web.

DDoS Attacks: By sending massive amounts of fake traffic to a website, bots can overwhelm servers, making the website inaccessible to legitimate users.

Automated Purchases: Bots are used to buy limited-edition products in bulk, which are then resold at a higher price, depriving genuine customers of the opportunity to purchase.

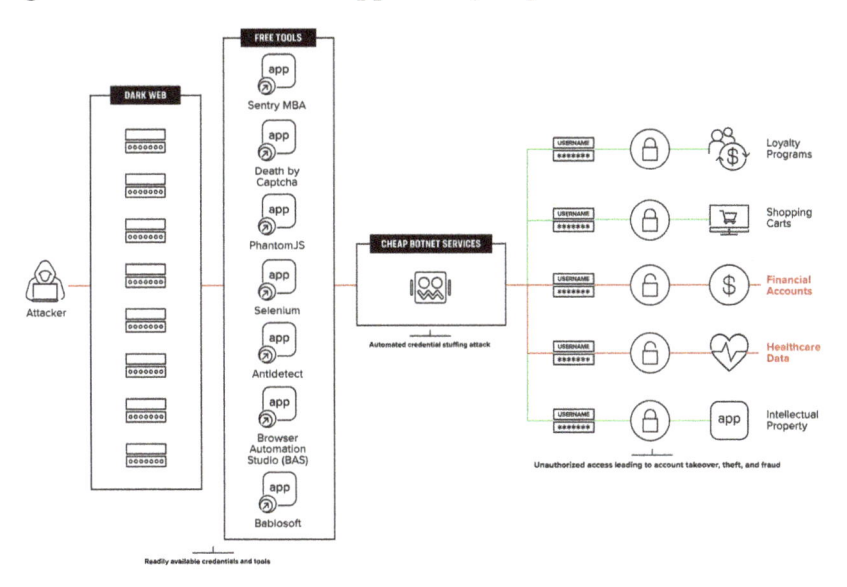

Credit : https://www.f5.com/resources/solution-guides/bot-detection-and-security

Beyond Firewalls: The Rise of Modern Cyber Threats

The Commercialization of Bot Attacks: The market for bot attacks has become highly commercialized, with a thriving underground economy that offers readymade botnets, tools, and services for anyone willing to pay. Here's how the bot attack market has evolved:

Botnets for Rent: Entire networks of compromised devices, known as botnets, are available for rent on the dark web. These botnets can be used to conduct a variety of attacks, such as DDoS or credential stuffing, without the attacker needing to build their own infrastructure.

Automation Tools: Tools allow attackers to automate the process of credential stuffing and other bot-driven activities. These tools are user-friendly and often come with configuration files tailored to specific websites, making it easy even for non-technical users to launch sophisticated attacks.

CAPTCHA Solvers and Anti-Fingerprinting: To bypass traditional defenses like CAPTCHAs, attackers use CAPTCHA-solving services, which employ machine learning or even human labor to solve challenges in real-time. Additionally, anti-fingerprinting tools help bots avoid detection by mimicking legitimate user behavior more convincingly.

Traditional Bot Detection: Where It Fails

Historically, bot detection relied on methods like CAPTCHAs and Multi-Factor Authentication (MFA) to differentiate between human users and bots. CAPTCHAs presented challenges that were difficult for bots to solve, such as identifying objects in images or solving puzzles, while MFA required additional verification steps, such as a code sent to a user's phone. However, these methods have significant drawbacks:

User Experience Impact: CAPTCHAs can frustrate legitimate users, leading to a poor user experience, especially when the challenges are difficult to solve or fail multiple times.

Bypassing Techniques: Advanced bots now use CAPTCHA-solving services and human labor to bypass these challenges, while MFA can be circumvented using phishing attacks or SIM swapping.

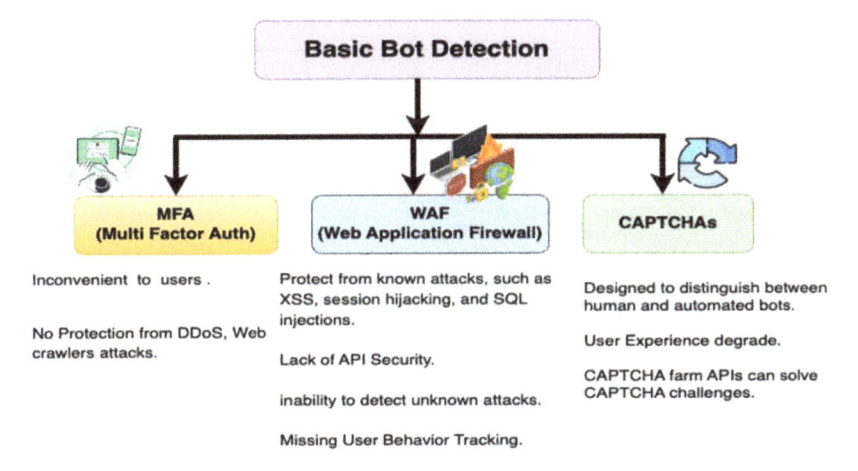

[Diagram: Basic Bot Detection]

MFA (Multi Factor Auth)
- Inconvenient to users.
- No Protection from DDoS, Web crawlers attacks.

WAF (Web Application Firewall)
- Protect from known attacks, such as XSS, session hijacking, and SQL injections.
- Lack of API Security.
- inability to detect unknown attacks.
- Missing User Behavior Tracking.

CAPTCHAs
- Designed to distinguish between human and automated bots.
- User Experience degrade.
- CAPTCHA farm APIs can solve CAPTCHA challenges.

The Need for Advanced Bot Detection

As bot attacks have grown more sophisticated, traditional detection methods have become less effective. The need for advanced bot detection solutions that employ machine learning, behavioral analysis, and real-time data processing has never been more critical. These modern tools are capable of adapting to evolving bot tactics, ensuring continuous protection while minimizing the impact on legitimate users.

Increasing Sophistication of Bot Attacks: Attackers are using more advanced techniques, making traditional detection methods, like CAPTCHAs, less effective.

Commercialization of Bot Attacks: The market for botnets and automated attack tools has expanded, making it easier for attackers to launch sophisticated bot attacks.

Necessity for Advanced Detection: Modern bot detection tools leverage machine learning, behavioral analysis, and real-time data processing to stay ahead of evolving bot strategies.

Maintaining User Trust: Advanced detection tools help safeguard digital assets and ensure a seamless user experience, preserving trust in online platforms.

Proactive Security Posture: Understanding the intent behind bot attacks and the limitations of traditional defenses underscores the need for implementing advanced detection technologies.

By understanding the intent behind bot attacks, the methods used by attackers, and the limitations of traditional defenses, organizations can better appreciate the need for and benefits of implementing advanced bot detection technologies. This proactive approach helps safeguard digital assets, maintain service integrity, and protect user trust in an increasingly hostile online environment.

False Positives vs. Negatives: The Hidden Costs

In the context of threat detection, When assessing the effectiveness of security tools, key metrics like False Rejection Rate (FRR) and False Acceptance Rate (FAR), alongside false positives and false negatives, are crucial.

False Positives: Occur when legitimate activity is wrongly flagged as malicious. This leads to unnecessary alerts, overwhelming security teams and diverting attention from genuine threats.

False Negatives: Happen when a real threat slips through undetected. These are critical, as they allow potential security breaches to go unnoticed, causing possible severe damage.

False Rejection Rate (FRR): Measures how often legitimate users are incorrectly denied access, which can frustrate users and hinder productivity.

False Acceptance Rate (FAR): Tracks how often unauthorized users gain access, posing a significant risk to the organization's security.

Striking the Right Balance:

Precision: Ensures that when the system raises an alert, it is likely to be accurate, thus reducing FAR and minimizing disruptions from false positives.

Recall: Focuses on capturing all potential threats, reducing FRR and ensuring that legitimate threats are not missed.

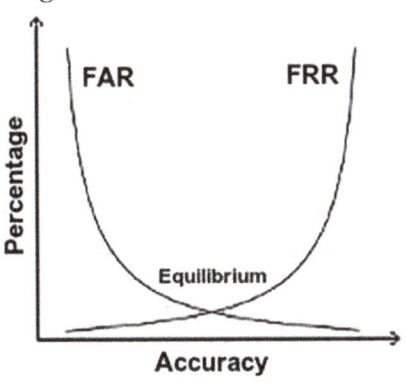

Image credit : https://www.bayometric.com/false-acceptance-rate-far-false-recognition-rate-frr/

Beyond Firewalls: The Rise of Modern Cyber Threats

Blind Spots in Insider Threat Detection

Traditional security measures like firewalls and Virtual Private Networks (VPNs) are highly effective at blocking unauthorized external access. However, they often fail to detect threats originating from within the organization, such as insider threats or the misuse of legitimate credentials. For example, an employee with authorized access may start downloading sensitive information after hours, but because the activity is coming from a trusted user, it goes unnoticed by perimeter defenses. This blind spot leaves organizations vulnerable to significant breaches that are difficult to detect and mitigate using traditional tools.

Static and Inflexible Risk Assessment

Intrusion Detection Systems (IDS) and similar tools often rely on predefined rules and thresholds to identify potential threats. While these systems can effectively block known threats, they struggle to adapt to new, sophisticated attack methods. For instance, if attackers use novel techniques that fall outside the expected patterns, the IDS might fail to trigger an alert, or worse, generate numerous false positives, leading to alert fatigue among security teams. This static nature of traditional risk assessments can cause organizations to miss emerging threats, leaving them vulnerable to attacks that evolve faster than the defenses in place.

Limited Scope in Identity and Access Management

Traditional cybersecurity heavily depends on managing user identities and access privileges through static methods like authentication logs, user profiles, and access control lists (ACLs). While these methods are essential for verifying user identities, they often fail to recognize when legitimate credentials are being used in malicious ways. For example, if an attacker gains access to an employee's login credentials, they can escalate their privileges and move laterally across the network without detection. This limitation in traditional access control mechanisms highlights the need for more dynamic and behavior-based security measures.

Lack of Pre-Decision Risk Awareness:

Traditional risk management approaches often base their assessments on historical data, assuming that past trends will predict future threats. This method fails to account for the dynamic nature of cyber threats, where attackers constantly develop new techniques and strategies. For instance, a company might decide to adopt a new cloud-based service without fully understanding the associated risks, simply because their past experiences have been positive. This oversight can lead to strategic decisions that expose the organization to vulnerabilities, such as sophisticated ransomware attacks targeting cloud infrastructure.

While firewalls, VPNs, and IDSs remain crucial components of any cybersecurity strategy, their limitations are evident in today's rapidly evolving threat landscape. Specifically:

Firewalls and VPNs effectively block unauthorized external access but are blind to the misuse of legitimate access.

Intrusion Detection Systems (IDS) rely on predefined rules that may not catch novel attack methods, leading to missed threats or alert fatigue.

Access control mechanisms are static, often failing to recognize when legitimate credentials are used in malicious ways.

Risk assessments based on past data may overlook emerging threats, leading to strategic decisions that leave the organization vulnerable.

Key Takeaways

	Firewalls and VPNs	Ineffective against misuse of legitimate access once attackers are inside.
	Intrusion Detection Systems (IDS)	Rule-Based Blind Spots.
	Static Access Control	Misses Credential Misuse; Lacks Behavioral Adaptability
	Risk Assessments	Fail to anticipate emerging threats, leading to outdated and vulnerable strategies.
	Lack of Insider Threat Detection	Overlooks risks posed by malicious insiders or compromised accounts, leaving critical gaps.
	False Positives	Legitimate activity wrongly flagged as a threat.
	False Negatives	Malicious activity that goes undetected.
	Botnets	Networks of compromised devices used for large-scale attacks.

Beyond Firewalls: *Security at Scale*

Conclusion:

As cyber threats continue to evolve and grow in complexity, traditional cybersecurity measures struggle to keep pace. Static access controls, outdated risk assessments, and basic insider threat detection are no longer sufficient to protect against today's dynamic and sophisticated attacks. Tools like firewalls, VPNs, and intrusion detection systems (IDS) were once the cornerstones of defense, but they now fall short, particularly in detecting insider threats, adapting to new attack vectors, and responding to changing behaviors.

This growing inadequacy highlights the need for more advanced, adaptive, and proactive cybersecurity strategies. The next chapter will delve into the cutting-edge tools and techniques that are reshaping the cybersecurity landscape, focusing on solutions like bot detection and fraud prevention that address these modern challenges head-on.

Reference:

https://www.fraud.com/post/fraud-risk-scoring

https://www.splunk.com/en_us/blog/learn/behavioral-analytics.html

https://www.crowdstrike.com/cybersecurity-101/secops/behavioral-analytics/

3

Cybersecurity Redefined: Beyond Traditional Defenses

The Need for Advanced Cybersecurity Tools:

As we've learned, cyberattacks have evolved into highly sophisticated and complex operations, rendering traditional security measures increasingly ineffective. In today's digital landscape, attackers deploy advanced tools and techniques that easily bypass conventional defenses, making it essential for organizations to adopt more innovative approaches. This chapter will explore cutting-edge cybersecurity tools that go beyond the basics, focusing on advanced strategies like bot detection and user behavior analysis. These technologies are crucial for preventing fraud, safeguarding digital assets, and maintaining a strong security posture in an ever-changing threat environment. By embracing these advanced solutions, businesses can stay one step ahead of cyber threats and ensure their defenses are both robust and resilient.

Endpoint Detection and Response (EDR) and Endpoint Security

Endpoint Detection and Response (EDR) is a cybersecurity technology designed to provide real-time monitoring, detection, and response capabilities for endpoint devices like laptops, desktops, and mobile devices. Unlike traditional antivirus software that mainly focuses on known threats, EDR offers a dynamic approach by continuously analyzing endpoint activities to detect potential threats, including those that might bypass conventional defenses. EDR is essential for identifying and responding to sophisticated attacks that target endpoints, ensuring that threats are mitigated before they can cause significant damage.

Endpoint Security Endpoint security acts as a vigilant guard at every digital entry point, combining preventive measures with real-time detection and response. Unlike traditional methods that rely solely on known threat signatures, modern endpoint security adapts to detect subtle signs of malicious activity. For instance, if an unfamiliar process starts on an endpoint, the system not only blocks it but also analyzes and responds, coordinating with other defenses to neutralize the threat.

Key Concepts of EDR and Endpoint Security

Continuous Monitoring and Data Collection: Both EDR and endpoint security solutions gather detailed data on activities across endpoint devices, including file operations, network connections, and process executions. This real-time monitoring is crucial for detecting anomalies and suspicious behavior early, before threats can cause significant harm.

Real-Time Threat Detection: Advanced algorithms and machine learning are utilized to analyze collected data, identifying anomalies such as unauthorized access patterns or abnormal network traffic. This real-time analysis helps detect threats that may bypass traditional defenses.

Patterns Analysis: Pattern analysis in EDR identifies irregular behaviors that differ from typical human activity. By examining factors like navigation paths, click patterns, and interaction timing, it effectively distinguishes bots from legitimate users, helping to secure digital platforms against automated attacks.

Automated Incident Response: Upon detecting potential threats, EDR and endpoint security systems can automatically isolate affected devices, terminate malicious processes, or roll back unauthorized changes. This rapid response is key to containing threats and minimizing damage.

Threat Hunting and Forensics: EDR tools provide detailed logs and forensic data, enabling proactive threat hunting and thorough investigation of security incidents. This helps in understanding the full scope of an attack and implementing measures to prevent future occurrences.

Cloud-Based Intelligence: Cloud-based endpoint security solutions enhance protection by continuously updating with the latest global threat intelligence. This ensures that endpoints are equipped to defend against emerging threats, adapting like a digital immune system to new challenges.

In summary, EDR and endpoint security work in tandem to provide a comprehensive, real-time defense against modern cyber threats, using continuous monitoring, behavioral analysis, and automated responses to safeguard digital assets.

Behavior Analysis in Cybersecurity: A Dynamic Approach to Threat Detection

Behavior analysis (BA) is a vital tool in modern cybersecurity, offering a proactive approach to detecting and mitigating threats by identifying deviations from normal behavior. Unlike traditional methods that rely on known threat signatures, BA uncovers potential security incidents by spotting unusual patterns, such as an employee accessing sensitive data at odd hours. This approach not only helps in early threat detection and response but also aids in meeting compliance requirements. However, BA does present challenges, including managing false positives, ensuring privacy, and integrating seamlessly with existing security systems.

Key Concepts of Behavior Analysis

Data Collection and Transformation: The first step in BA involves collecting relevant data from sources like network traffic logs, access logs, and user activity records. This data is then transformed into a suitable format for analysis. Modern BA systems automate this process, enabling real-time data extraction and transformation. For instance, network traffic logs might reveal typical data flows across an organization, while access logs provide insights into resource access patterns.

- **Data Analysis and Anomaly Detection:** Once data is prepared, unsupervised machine learning algorithms analyze it to detect anomalies—patterns that deviate from established baselines. These algorithms are particularly effective in identifying unknown threats, such as a user logging in from an unusual location, indicating a potential security breach.

Behaviour Analysis Data Source

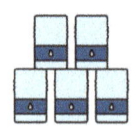

Identity Trails | Device Records | DNS logs | User Activity | Network Activity

Alerting and Remediation: When an anomaly is detected, the BA system alerts the security team, providing the necessary information to respond quickly. Actions might include locking accounts, blocking access, or initiating further investigation to address potential threats before they cause significant damage.

Continuous Learning: BA systems continuously learn and adapt to new behaviors and emerging threats. This ongoing process refines detection capabilities, reducing false positives and negatives, and improving the accuracy of threat detection over time.

Behavior Analysis in Action: UEBA, NBA, and ITBA

User and Entity Behavior Analytics (UEBA): UEBA plays a crucial role in modern cybersecurity by analyzing the behavior of users and devices within a network to detect anomalies that could indicate security breaches. Unlike traditional security measures that depend on known threat signatures, UEBA continuously monitors normal activities, establishing behavioral baselines for each entity—whether a user or a device. It then compares ongoing actions against these baselines to identify deviations, such as unusual login times or unexpected data transfers, that may signal insider threats, brute-force attacks, or compromised accounts. This proactive approach enables organizations to detect and respond to sophisticated attacks early, reducing the risk of major security incidents. The key benefits of UEBA include identifying unknown and emerging threats, automating data analysis to ease the workload on security teams, and providing actionable insights that enhance operational efficiency.

Network Behavior Analytics (NBA): NBA focuses on monitoring network traffic to detect unusual activity, such as unexpected spikes in data transfer or communication with known malicious sites. This capability is crucial for identifying threats like Distributed Denial of Service (DDoS) attacks, where the network is flooded with traffic to overwhelm and disable services. By continuously analyzing network patterns, NBA helps organizations spot and mitigate these types of attacks before they cause significant disruption.

Insider Threat Behavior Analytics (ITBA): ITBA, a specialized subset of UEBA, targets internal threats by identifying suspicious behaviors from trusted insiders. This includes monitoring for significant changes in an employee's access patterns or activities that deviate from their typical behavior. For example, if an employee suddenly attempts to access sensitive data or systems outside their usual scope of work, ITBA can flag this as a potential insider threat, allowing for prompt investigation and response.

Behavior analysis (BA) is essential in modern cybersecurity, offering proactive threat detection and the ability to identify advanced persistent threats (APTs). BA helps organizations meet compliance requirements by monitoring user activity and preventing unauthorized access to sensitive data. However, it also presents challenges, including managing false positives, addressing privacy concerns, and integrating BA tools within existing security frameworks. Despite these challenges, BA remains vital for safeguarding digital environments, continuously adapting to detect and neutralize threats before they can cause significant damage.

Anomaly Detection

Anomaly detection is a powerful technique in cybersecurity, particularly when it comes to identifying potential fraud. By leveraging machine learning models, organizations can detect unusual patterns that deviate from normal user behavior, which may indicate fraudulent activity. Following are the

Anamoly Detection Learning Models

Unsupervised Learning Models: These models are highly effective in fraud detection because they don't rely on labeled datasets. Instead, they identify outliers by learning what constitutes typical user behavior over time. For example, clustering algorithms can group normal login behaviors, and any deviation from these clusters can be flagged as suspicious.

Supervised Learning Models: When historical data is available, supervised models can classify actions as either legitimate or fraudulent. Techniques like Random Forests or Neural Networks can be employed to predict the likelihood of a fraud attempt based on past login data.

Outlier Detection: In the context of login activity, outlier detection can be particularly useful. For instance, if a user suddenly logs in from an unusual geographic location or at an odd time of day that deviates from their typical pattern, the system can flag this as a potential fraud attempt. By catching these anomalies, organizations can prompt additional security measures, such as multi-factor authentication, to prevent unauthorized access.

Anomaly detection in fraud prevention is about identifying unusual patterns in user behavior that might indicate fraudulent activity. The process involves collecting and analyzing data from various sources, like transaction history, geographical location, device information, and user behavior, to spot anything out of the ordinary.

Key Steps of Anamoly Detection:

Data Collection: The system gathers data such as transaction history, location, device details, and user behavior patterns.

Decision Points: The collected data is compared against specific criteria, like unusual transaction sizes or unfamiliar login locations, to identify potential risks.

Scoring and Risk Assessment: Each criterion is given a weight, and the data is scored to determine the overall fraud risk. For example, a small, local transaction might get a low score, while a large, international transaction from a new device could get a high score.

Actions Based on Scores: Depending on the score, the system takes different actions:

- Low Score: The transaction proceeds as normal.
- Medium Score: Additional verification might be required.
- High Score: The transaction is flagged for review or blocked.

Real-World Example: Detecting Fraudulent Logins: Imagine a scenario where a user's account is typically accessed from the same device in New York. If there's a sudden login attempt from a device in another country, especially during odd hours, an anomaly detection model would flag this as suspicious. The system could then take actions like temporarily locking the account or requiring additional verification to ensure that the login is legitimate.

By using machine learning to detect anomalies, this system can effectively identify and prevent fraudulent activities while minimizing disruptions for legitimate users.

Deception Technology:

In the world of cybersecurity, deception technology emerges as a sophisticated strategy, akin to setting traps for intruders in a maze of false leads. It is designed to detect, analyze, and thwart advanced threats by luring attackers into interacting with decoy assets that appear legitimate but are, in fact, designed to deceive. This technology not only confuses and misleads attackers but also provides critical early warning signs of potential breaches, allowing organizations to respond swiftly.

Deception technology involves the deployment of false assets—such as servers, applications, credentials, or user accounts—within an organization's network. These decoys are indistinguishable from real assets and are strategically placed to attract attackers who have bypassed traditional security defenses. The moment an attacker engages with these decoys, the system triggers alerts, enabling security teams to identify and respond to the threat.

For instance, consider a scenario where an attacker gains access to a network and begins scanning for vulnerable systems. A honeypot, a type of deception technology, mimics a vulnerable server. Once the attacker interacts with it, the system logs the activity and raises an alert, revealing the intruder's presence. This interaction not only disrupts the attacker's progress but also provides valuable insights into their tactics, techniques, and procedures.

How Deception Technology Works

Deception technology operates on a principle similar to that of setting up elaborate traps. It creates an environment rich with decoy assets that look, feel, and behave like genuine network resources. These decoys are carefully designed to be enticing targets for attackers, who are likely to engage with them under the assumption that they are interacting with valuable assets.

The deployment of deception technology typically involves the following steps:

Creation of Decoy Assets: These can include fake servers, user accounts, credentials, and even entire networks that are indistinguishable from real assets. The goal is to create an environment where any unauthorized interaction with these assets is immediately suspicious.

Monitoring and Alerting: The system continuously monitors the decoys for any signs of interaction. Since legitimate users have no reason to interact with these decoys, any activity is treated as potentially malicious. The moment an attacker engages with a decoy, an alert is triggered, providing security teams with real-time information about the threat.

Analysis and Response: Once an alert is triggered, the system collects detailed information about the attack, such as the attacker's methods and tools. This information is invaluable for understanding the threat and formulating a response. In some cases, the system may automatically initiate response actions, such as isolating the affected part of the network or redirecting the attacker to a controlled environment where they can be studied further.

Types of Deception Technologies

There are various forms of deception technology, each serving a specific purpose:

Honeypots: These are decoy systems that mimic real servers or applications. Honeypots are used to attract attackers and gather information about their methods.

Honey Users and Honey Credentials: These are fake user accounts and credentials designed to detect unauthorized access attempts. For example, an attacker might use brute-force techniques to guess passwords. If they attempt to access a honey user account, the system detects the activity and alerts the security team.

Honey Tokens: These are small pieces of information, such as fake API keys or database records, planted within the network. If an attacker tries to use or exfiltrate a honey token, it signals that a breach has occurred.

The Strategic Importance of Deception Technology

Deception technology shifts the burden onto attackers by turning the network into a minefield of decoys, making it much harder to carry out attacks undetected. It provides early threat detection, reduces false positives, and offers valuable insights into attacker behavior, complementing traditional defenses. By creating a hostile environment, deception technology delays and frustrates attackers, giving defenders crucial time to respond and mitigate threats before they cause significant damage.

Threat Intelligence Platforms:

Threat Intelligence Platforms (TIPs) are essential in today's cybersecurity landscape, offering proactive defense by actively gathering and analyzing data from various sources to predict and prevent cyber threats. Serving as a central hub, TIPs collect, process, and transform raw information into actionable insights that help organizations stay ahead of potential risks. These platforms seamlessly integrate with existing security systems like firewalls, Endpoint Detection and Response (EDR) tools, and Security Information and Event Management (SIEM) systems, thereby enhancing overall security measures. By continuously monitoring for signs of danger, TIPs provide real-time alerts and detailed threat analysis, enabling security teams to respond swiftly and effectively to potential cyberattacks. This integration and real-time detection significantly bolster an organization's ability to protect its digital assets, ensuring a stronger security posture in the face of increasingly sophisticated threats.

How Does a Threat Intelligence Platform Work?

The functionality of a TIP revolves around several key processes:

Data Collection and Aggregation: TIPs gather threat intelligence from a multitude of sources, both internal and external. This can include data from open-source threat feeds, commercial threat intelligence providers, and internal logs. The platform aggregates this data to provide a comprehensive view of the current threat landscape.

Normalization and Deduplication: Given that threat data comes in various formats and may include redundant information, TIPs normalize this data into a consistent format and remove duplicates. This step is crucial for ensuring that the analysis is based on accurate and relevant data.

Processing and Analysis: Once the data is collected and cleaned, the TIP processes it to extract meaningful insights. For instance, it may identify Indicators of Compromise (IoCs) such as malicious IP addresses or domain names, which can be used to detect and block threats in real-time.

Integration with Security Systems: A TIP doesn't work in isolation. It integrates with the organization's existing security infrastructure, such as firewalls, EDR, and SIEM systems, to automatically distribute threat intelligence across the network. This ensures that all security measures are informed by the latest data, enabling a coordinated and rapid response to emerging threats.

As cyber threats become more sophisticated and diverse, the need for robust threat intelligence capabilities is more critical than ever. Threat Intelligence Platforms provide organizations with the tools they need to stay ahead of attackers, transforming raw data into actionable insights that strengthen defenses and reduce risk. By integrating TIPs into their security strategies, organizations can ensure that they are equipped to face the challenges of the modern cyber threat landscape.

Key Takeaways

	Necessity of Advanced Tools	Traditional defenses are insufficient; advanced tools are vital for modern threat detection
	Endpoint Detection and Response	EDR continuously monitors and responds to threats on endpoint devices in real-time.
	User and Entity Behavior Analytics	UEBA detects anomalies in user and device behavior, identifying potential threats.
	Deception Technology	Lures attackers into interacting with decoys, providing early detection and response.
	Threat Intelligence Platforms	TIPs gather and analyze threat data, providing actionable insights for preemptive defense.

Building Next-Generation Cyber defense:

As we dive into the technical foundations of advanced cybersecurity tools, this section will reveal the intricate workings behind essential defenses like bot detection, user behavior analytics, honeypots, and threat intelligence platforms. These tools are not just technological marvels; they are the guardians of our digital world, built on the principles of artificial intelligence, machine learning, and real-time data analysis. In this section, you'll gain insight into how these systems are engineered to anticipate and neutralize sophisticated cyber threats, laying the groundwork for a deeper understanding of how these cutting-edge technologies operate and protect us in an increasingly complex digital landscape.

Designing Bot Detection Systems

Bot detection is a critical component of modern cybersecurity, focusing on identifying and blocking malicious bot activities while ensuring seamless interaction for legitimate users. The process involves several sophisticated techniques, each contributing to the overall effectiveness of bot detection systems.

Bot Detection Tool in action:

In this section, we delve into the technical components of building a bot detection tool that can effectively counter these advanced threats. By understanding the underlying mechanics of bot detection, including data collection, feature extraction, and real-time analysis, we can create robust defenses that adapt to the evolving threat landscape.

Beyond Firewalls: *Security at Scale*

Data Collection and Feature Extraction:

The foundation of any bot detection system lies in the data it collects and the features it extracts from that data. This process involves gathering detailed information from various sources, which can then be analyzed to distinguish between bots and human users.

HTTP Request Data: Web servers like Nginx and Apache are configured to log every HTTP request, capturing critical data such as user-agent strings, referrer URLs, cookies, and session tokens. Analyzing this data can reveal patterns indicative of bot activity. For instance, if a specific user-agent string is used repeatedly across different sessions or if certain headers are missing, it can be a strong indicator of bot traffic.

Device Fingerprinting: Tools like FingerprintJS collect a wide range of device attributes, such as screen resolution, installed fonts, time zone, and browser plugins. By combining these attributes, a unique fingerprint can be generated for each device. For example, if multiple requests with the same fingerprint but different IP addresses are detected, this could indicate that a botnet is at work.

Behavioral Metrics: By deploying JavaScript on web pages, bot detection systems can capture real-time user interaction data, such as mouse movements, click patterns, and typing speed. Anomalies in these metrics, like uniform mouse movements or rapid, consistent keystrokes, can signal the presence of a bot. A human user typically exhibits more varied and nuanced behavior, making these patterns a reliable indicator of automated activity.

Velocity Data: Velocity data tracks the frequency and speed of requests made by an individual user. High velocity in making requests, such as repeated login attempts within a short period, can indicate automated behavior. Tools like Akamai's Bot Manager use velocity metrics to detect and mitigate bots by flagging excessive request rates that diverge from typical human behavior.

IP ASN Data: Analyzing Autonomous System Numbers (ASN) associated with IP addresses helps in identifying potential bot activity. For example, a spike in traffic from an ASN known to host botnets or data centers can be a red flag. Bot detection systems like Distil Networks integrate IP ASN data to enhance detection accuracy by correlating it with other data points, such as geolocation and velocity.

Network Data: Utilizing tools like MaxMind GeoIP, bot detection systems can analyze the geolocation of IP addresses. Bots often use IP addresses from data centers, proxies, or VPNs, which can be flagged if they don't match the expected geographic distribution of legitimate users. For instance, multiple login attempts from an IP associated with a known data center might be indicative of a bot attack.

AI-BOT DETECION

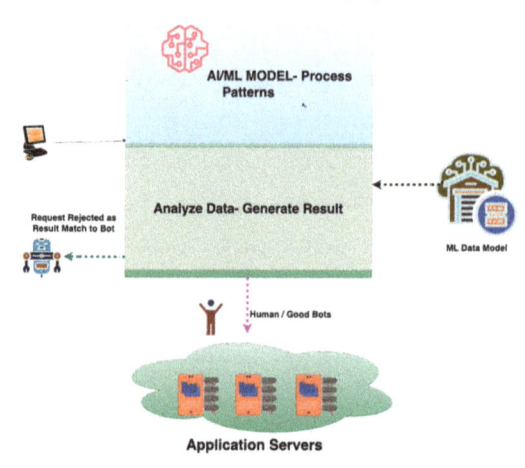

Scoring Mechanism

Once data is collected, it needs to be evaluated using a scoring mechanism that assigns a risk level to each session or interaction.

Anomaly Detection: Python libraries like Scikit-learn can be employed to implement anomaly detection algorithms that analyze user behavior in real time. For instance, if a particular session shows a high frequency of requests that deviate from normal user patterns, it may be assigned a high risk score.

Statistical Models: Using statistical tools like R or MATLAB, developers can create models that establish baseline behavior patterns and identify deviations. For example, if the number of requests per minute from a single IP address suddenly spikes, it could be indicative of a bot attempting a Distributed Denial of Service (DDoS) attack.

Heuristic Analysis: Elasticsearch and Kibana can be used to apply heuristic rules that flag known bot behaviors, such as repetitive access to specific URLs or the use of certain user-agent strings. For example, if a user-agent string is identified as belonging to a known bot framework like PhantomJS, the session can be flagged for further inspection.

Machine Learning Integration: Machine learning is key to modern bot detection, adapting to new behaviors. Supervised learning, like Random Forests, classifies traffic as bot or human by analyzing known patterns. Unsupervised learning, such as k-means clustering, identifies new bot activity by grouping similar sessions. Neural networks, using tools like TensorFlow, detect automation in complex data, enhancing bot detection accuracy.

Real-Time Scoring and Response

Real-time analysis and response are critical for effective bot detection, ensuring that threats are mitigated before they can cause harm.

Real-Time API Calls: Using services like IPinfo or VirusTotal, the system can query external threat intelligence databases to check the reputation of an IP address or domain in real-time. For example, if a session originates from an IP associated with a botnet, the system can immediately block access or prompt further verification.

Dynamic Content Serving: With Nginx or HAProxy, bot detection systems can serve different content based on the calculated risk score. For example, high-risk sessions might be presented with a CAPTCHA or a reduced feature set to mitigate the potential impact of bot activity.

Automated Response: Using automation frameworks like Ansible or SaltStack, the system can automatically isolate suspicious IP addresses or terminate malicious sessions. For example, if a bot is detected attempting to brute force login credentials, the system can automatically block the IP address and notify the security team.

Continuous Improvement: Essential for maintaining effective bot detection as threats evolve.

Log Analysis: Use tools like Splunk for retrospective analysis to identify and refine detection methods.

Adaptive Learning: Regularly retrain models with new data to stay effective against new threats.

Beyond Firewalls: *Security at Scale*

Feedback Loops: Integrate with SIEM systems to keep detection mechanisms updated and resilient.

Building a robust bot detection tool is vital for protecting digital platforms from sophisticated automated threats. By integrating advanced data collection, such as behavioral analysis and IP tracking, with machine learning, organizations can effectively distinguish between legitimate users and harmful bots, enhancing security and user experience. For small to mid-sized businesses, using third-party endpoint security solutions offers a practical way to implement these defenses without requiring extensive internal resources. As cyber threats evolve, proactive bot detection is essential for ensuring long-term digital resilience and success.

Designing Behavioral Analysis Tools

Behavioral analysis tools are an integral part of modern cybersecurity, designed to detect anomalies by analyzing user behaviors across various platforms. These tools are essential for identifying potential fraudulent activities that deviate from established behavioral norms. While they share some similarities with bot detection systems, behavioral analysis tools focus more on human interactions and subtle deviations from normal behavior, making them particularly effective for detecting sophisticated fraud attempts that might slip through more traditional security measures.

Data Collection and Feature Extraction

The foundation of behavioral analysis lies in comprehensive data collection. Unlike bot detection systems that primarily focus on network traffic and browser characteristics, behavioral analysis tools gather a broader spectrum of data points, including:

User Interaction Data: This includes tracking mouse movements, typing patterns, and click behaviors. For example, a user who typically navigates a website in a specific way suddenly deviating from this pattern might trigger an alert.

Transactional Data: By monitoring transaction history, the system can detect anomalies such as sudden increases in transaction size, frequency, or changes in payment methods. For instance, a user who consistently makes small purchases but suddenly begins making large transactions could indicate fraud.

Geolocation Data: Tracking the geographic origin of user actions can highlight inconsistencies, such as logins from unusual locations. If a user logs in from New York but, within minutes, attempts a transaction from Tokyo, this could signal a compromised account.

Device and Network Data: While bot detection focuses on identifying automated systems, behavioral analysis tools look at the devices and networks used. Sudden changes in the device or network type—such as switching from a known home network to a public Wi-Fi network—can also be red flags.

Pattern Recognition and Anomaly Detection

Once data is collected, the system builds a profile of normal user behavior using machine learning algorithms. This process involves several steps:

Baseline Establishment: Initially, the system observes user behavior to establish what constitutes "normal" activity for each individual. For example, if a user typically logs in during business hours and from a specific location, this becomes part of their baseline.

Continuous Monitoring: The system continuously monitors ongoing user activities, comparing them against the established baseline. Unlike bot detection, which often identifies immediate threats, behavioral analysis is more focused on long-term patterns and subtle changes over time.

Anomaly Scoring: When deviations occur, the system assigns a risk score based on the severity and frequency of the anomaly. For instance, a single login from a new device might generate a low score, while multiple suspicious activities within a short period would result in a higher score.

Real-Time Alerts: If the risk score exceeds a certain threshold, the system triggers an alert for further investigation. For example, if a user suddenly starts transferring large amounts of money from an account, this action would prompt an immediate review.

Adaptive Machine Learning Models

Behavioral analysis tools leverage advanced machine learning models that evolve with the user's behavior:

Supervised and Unsupervised Learning: Initially, supervised learning models help the system recognize known patterns of fraud. As more data is collected, unsupervised learning models adapt to new patterns that may not have been previously identified.

Contextual Learning: These models consider the context of user actions, making them more accurate over time. For example, purchasing activity during a holiday season might be flagged as suspicious if it deviates significantly from the user's usual behavior, but contextual learning would account for seasonal changes.

Feedback Loops: User feedback on false positives or confirmed fraud cases helps refine the models. This continuous learning process ensures that the system becomes increasingly effective at detecting fraud while minimizing disruptions to legitimate users.

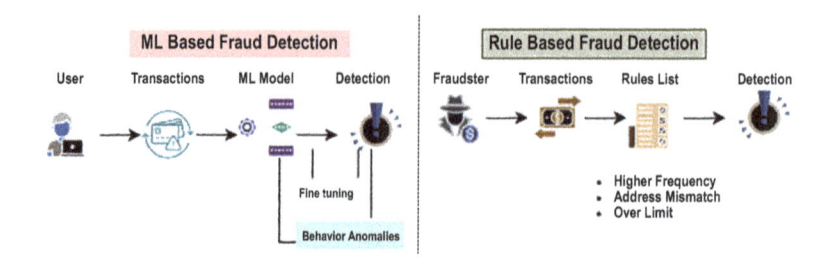

The Benefits of Behavioral Fraud Detection

Behavioral fraud detection offers several key advantages:

Early Detection: By identifying deviations from normal behavior, the system can catch fraud early, often before any significant damage is done.

Reduced False Positives: Traditional rule-based systems often trigger numerous false alarms, but behavioral analysis is more precise, minimizing disruptions to legitimate users.

Adaptability: As fraudsters develop new tactics, behavioral fraud detection systems continuously learn and adapt, making it increasingly difficult for criminals to succeed.

Enhanced User Experience: By tailoring security measures to individual behaviors, businesses can offer strong protection without compromising the customer experience.

Bot Detection vs. Behavior Analysis: What Sets Them Apart

While both behavioral analysis and bot detection systems aim to protect against cyber threats, their approaches and focus areas differ significantly:

Focus on Human Behavior: Behavioral analysis tools are designed to monitor and understand human behavior, looking for subtle deviations that indicate fraud. This contrasts with bot detection, which primarily identifies non-human activity by analyzing network traffic and browser characteristics.

Long-Term Analysis vs. Immediate Detection: Bot detection systems often provide real-time protection by identifying and blocking automated threats as they occur. In contrast, behavioral analysis tools may operate over longer periods, identifying fraud based on gradual changes in user behavior.

User-Centric Approach: Behavioral analysis is more user-centric, focusing on individual user profiles and personal patterns. This is different from bot detection, which often involves analyzing larger-scale patterns across many users to identify automated scripts or botnets.

Cybersecurity Redefined: Beyond Traditional Defenses

Challenges and Considerations in Implementing Behavioral Fraud Detection

Implementing behavioral fraud detection systems presents several challenges that organizations must address to ensure effectiveness while minimizing risks.

Data Privacy Concerns: The vast amount of data collected for behavioral analysis raises significant privacy issues. Tracking user interactions, transactions, and personal information requires strict compliance with data protection regulations like GDPR or CCPA. Organizations must implement robust encryption and anonymization techniques to safeguard sensitive information while maintaining transparency about data usage.

Complex Implementation: Deploying behavioral fraud detection systems is technically challenging. It involves integrating various data sources, setting up machine learning models, and continuously updating the system to adapt to new threats. Smaller organizations may struggle with the resources and expertise needed for effective implementation and maintenance. Continuous monitoring and fine-tuning of algorithms are necessary to prevent them from becoming outdated or ineffective.

Adapting to Behavior Changes: User behavior evolves over time due to changing habits, new technologies, or demographic shifts. Behavioral analysis systems must adapt to these changes to remain accurate. Continuous monitoring and periodic retraining of machine learning models are required to ensure the system aligns with current user behavior patterns and avoids increased false positives or missed fraudulent activities.

Dependence on Data Quality: The success of behavioral fraud detection relies heavily on data quality. Incomplete, inaccurate, or outdated data can lead to errors, such as undetected fraud or excessive false positives. Ensuring that data is clean, comprehensive, and up-to-date is crucial. Organizations must invest in data quality management practices, including regular audits and validation processes, to maintain the integrity of the data used for analysis.

Designing Honeypots

Honeypots serve as a strategic decoy in cybersecurity, designed to attract attackers and study their methods without putting critical assets at risk. These systems mimic legitimate environments, luring cybercriminals into a controlled setup where their tactics can be observed and analyzed. Here's an exploration of how to technically implement honeypots, using real-life examples to highlight their effectiveness.

Designing a Convincing Honeypot Environment: To deceive attackers, a honeypot must appear to be a legitimate system. It should simulate a production environment closely, running processes and services that attackers would expect to find on a real server.

Mimicking Real Systems: A successful honeypot must look like an authentic target. This involves setting up the honeypot with an operating system, running common services (like FTP, SSH, or HTTP), and populating it with realistic but non-sensitive data. For instance, a honeypot mimicking a financial server might include fake transaction records or customer data.

Example: A research team at a university deployed a high-interaction honeypot that simulated a financial database. This setup attracted attackers who believed they had found a valuable target. The system logged all their actions, providing insights into new SQL injection techniques.

Deploying Honeypots in the Network: Placement of the honeypot within the network is critical. It should be accessible enough to attract attackers but isolated to prevent them from pivoting to real systems. Positioning the honeypot within a demilitarized zone (DMZ) or behind a firewall with strict rules ensures that even if compromised, the honeypot cannot be used as a launchpad for further attacks.

Example: A company positioned a honeypot in their DMZ, configured to simulate a web server vulnerable to known exploits. This honeypot detected a series of automated attacks targeting outdated software, allowing the security team to update their real servers preemptively.

Advanced Logging and Sniffing: Intrusion Detection Systems (IDS) like Snort can be integrated with the honeypot to monitor all traffic and log every interaction. Custom scripts can also be written to log specific actions, such as attempts to access certain files or execute commands. These logs are crucial for forensic analysis, helping to reconstruct the attack and understand the tools used.

Behavioral Analysis of Attackers: Honeypots also allow for the analysis of attacker behavior in a controlled environment. By monitoring how attackers interact with the system—whether they try to elevate privileges, which files they attempt to access, or how they move laterally within the network—security teams can gain insights into emerging threats.

Beyond Firewalls: *Security at Scale*

Example: A high-interaction honeypot set up in a hospital's network was able to track an attacker's movement as they tried to pivot from the honeypot to the hospital's real patient data servers. The behavioral analysis indicated that the attacker was testing for lateral movement capabilities, which led the security team to reinforce their segmentation and access controls.

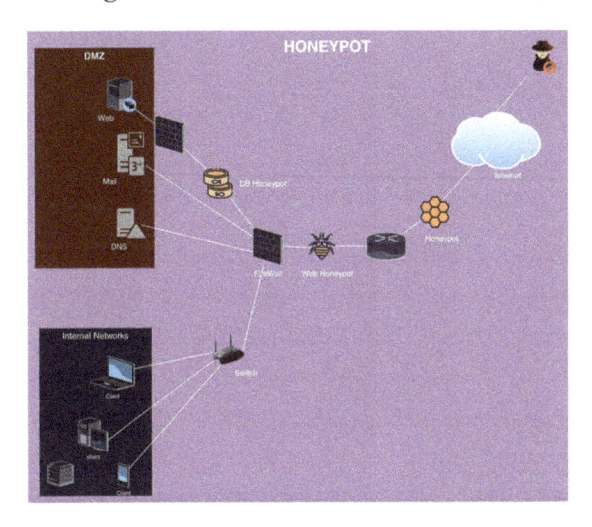

Monitoring and Analyzing Attacker Behavior: Honeypots are only as valuable as the data they collect. Detailed logging and analysis are essential to understanding the attacker's methods and improving overall security.

Different Types of Honeypots and Their Use Cases

Honeypots come in various forms, each designed to serve different purposes and target different types of threats. Their complexity can range from simple setups meant to attract basic automated attacks to sophisticated environments that engage attackers in long-term interactions, providing valuable insights into their techniques and strategies.

Low-Interaction Honeypots: These are designed to emulate a limited number of services and applications. They are easier to deploy and maintain and are primarily used to detect and log basic automated attacks, such as port scanning or simple network probes. For example, a low-interaction honeypot might simulate a common service like FTP or HTTP, attracting automated bots that scan the internet for vulnerable systems. Tools like Honeytrap and KFsensor are popular examples of low-interaction honeypots.

High-Interaction Honeypots: These honeypots mimic full production systems, including operating systems, applications, and network services. They allow attackers to interact more deeply with the environment, providing richer data on attacker behavior and techniques. High-interaction honeypots are more resource-intensive but offer more detailed insights. For instance, a high-interaction honeypot could simulate an entire enterprise environment, complete with databases, web servers, and user accounts, allowing researchers to study sophisticated attacks like APTs (Advanced Persistent Threats). Honeynets, which are networks of high-interaction honeypots, are used to observe how attackers move laterally within a network.

Malware Honeypots: These honeypots are designed to attract and capture malware by simulating vulnerable devices or software. For example, a malware honeypot might emulate a USB storage device to attract malware that spreads via removable media. Once the malware is captured, security researchers can analyze its behavior and develop countermeasures. Tools like Ghost are examples of malware honeypots.

Spam Honeypots: These honeypots simulate open mail relays or vulnerable email servers to attract and study spammers. When spammers attempt to send test emails to these honeypots, the system logs their activities, helping organizations understand and block spam campaigns. Spam honeypots are useful for developing anti-spam technologies and for monitoring the techniques used by spammers to bypass filters.

Spider Honeypots: These honeypots are specifically designed to lure and trap web crawlers and spiders who attempt to harvest sensitive information from web applications.

Database Honeypots: These honeypots are configured to resemble vulnerable databases, such as those susceptible to SQL injection attacks. Attackers are lured into attempting to exploit these databases, allowing defenders to observe their methods and improve their database security measures. Honeypots that emulate SQL databases are particularly effective in attracting attackers looking to steal sensitive information like credit card details.

Research vs. Production Honeypots: Research Honeypots are primarily used in academic or research settings to study new types of attacks and to gather intelligence on emerging threats. They tend to be high-interaction and are deployed in controlled environments where they can capture detailed information about attacker methods and tools. Production Honeypots are deployed within a live environment and are used to detect and respond to active threats within an organization. They provide additional layers of monitoring and detection, complementing traditional security measures like firewalls and intrusion detection systems.

Honeynets: Rather than being a single system, a honeynet is a network of honeypots designed to observe an attacker's behavior across multiple systems. Honeynets are used to study how attackers move within a network after gaining initial access, providing valuable insights into lateral movement, privilege escalation, and other advanced attack techniques.

Challenges and Ethical Considerations

While honeypots offer valuable insights, they come with challenges, including maintenance, false positives, and ethical concerns.

Maintenance and False Positives: Maintaining a honeypot involves ensuring it remains convincing to attackers and that it doesn't become an easy target for exploitation. Regular updates and careful monitoring are necessary to keep the honeypot effective and to minimize false positives in the logs.

Example: A security team running a high-interaction honeypot for over a year found that the honeypot started attracting fewer attacks. After investigating, they realized that the services and software needed updates to reflect current vulnerabilities, as attackers were likely bypassing the honeypot for more current targets.

Ethical and Legal Issues: Deploying honeypots raises ethical and legal questions, particularly regarding the collection of data on attackers. It's essential to ensure that the honeypot complies with legal regulations and ethical guidelines, avoiding any actions that could be construed as entrapment or unauthorized surveillance.

Example: A financial institution deployed a honeypot designed to attract attackers targeting online banking systems. Before deployment, the institution consulted with legal experts to ensure that the honeypot's data collection methods complied with GDPR and other relevant regulations, ensuring that the system was legally sound.

Honeypots are a critical component in modern cybersecurity, offering a unique opportunity to study attacker methods in a controlled environment. By carefully designing, deploying, and maintaining honeypots, organizations can gain invaluable insights into the tactics used by cybercriminals and enhance their overall security posture. However, the implementation of honeypots must be approached with careful consideration of both technical challenges and ethical implications, ensuring that they serve as an effective, responsible tool in the broader cybersecurity strategy.

Designing Threat Intelligence Platform (TIP)

Implementing a Threat Intelligence Platform (TIP) is an intricate process that requires meticulous integration of various technical components to enhance an organization's ability to detect, analyze, and respond to cyber threats effectively. This process involves several key steps, each vital for ensuring that the TIP functions optimally.

Data Ingestion and Integration: A robust TIP must be capable of gathering data from a wide array of sources, both external and internal. For example, integrating commercial threat feeds like those from FireEye or Recorded Future can provide valuable insights into emerging threats. Additionally, internal telemetry sources, such as Security Information and Event Management (SIEM) systems, which aggregate log data from firewalls and intrusion detection systems, are crucial for comprehensive threat monitoring. By leveraging data streaming tools like Apache Kafka, the TIP can ensure that this data is ingested and processed in near real-time, allowing for timely threat detection. Threat intelligence feeds gather data from a variety of sources, each serving different purposes depending on the **type of feed**.

- **Commercial Threat Intelligence:** These feeds collect anonymized data from customer networks and analyze it to identify potential threats and trends. They are often provided by vendors supplying commercial security devices.

- **Open Source Intelligence (OSINT):** OSINT gathers information from publicly available sources such as websites, social media, and public forums. However, these feeds can overlap with commercial feeds, potentially duplicating data.

- **Government Intelligence:** Government agencies provide feeds that can benefit both public and private sectors, but they may duplicate information already available in commercial feeds.

- **Industry-Specific Feeds:** These are tailored to specific sectors, offering unique insights relevant to particular industries, such as critical infrastructure.

- **Third-Party Threat Intelligence:** These feeds offer real-time data on threats like DDoS attacks, malware, and botnets, aiding in rapid threat identification and mitigation.

- **Local Intelligence:** Organizations should also collect and analyze their own internal logs and security events. Combining local intelligence with external feeds ensures comprehensive threat coverage and more accurate detection.

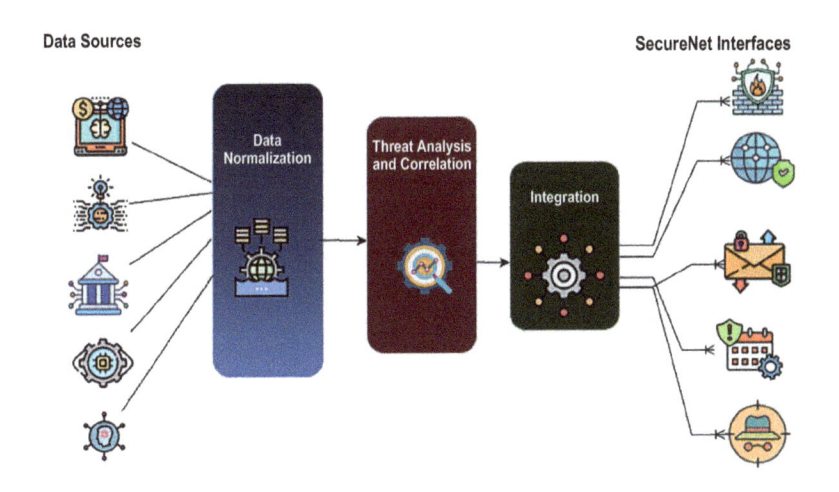

Data Normalization and Enrichment are crucial for making the information actionable. This involves converting data from various sources into a consistent format and enhancing it with additional context. For instance, a TIP might receive a raw IP address from a SIEM log, which is then enriched by cross-referencing it with services like VirusTotal to determine if the IP is associated with known malicious activities. Using ETL (Extract, Transform, Load) processes, such as those provided by Apache NiFi, can automate the transformation of disparate data into a structured format, ready for analysis.

Threat Analysis and Correlation: TIP applies machine learning algorithms and advanced correlation techniques to identify potential threats. For example, if the TIP detects a pattern of failed login attempts followed by a successful login, it might correlate this with known threat indicators, revealing a potential credential-stuffing attack. By utilizing machine learning frameworks like TensorFlow, the TIP can train models to recognize such patterns, continuously improving its threat detection capabilities. Correlation engines further enhance this process by linking seemingly unrelated data points, such as associating a suspicious domain name with known malware, to identify broader attack campaigns.

Automated Response and Integration with Security Tools is another critical aspect of a well-implemented TIP. Upon detecting a threat, the TIP should be able to trigger automated responses by interfacing with other security tools.

Integrating Advance Tools with Traditional Cybersecurity

Bot Detection and Endpoint Protection

- **Deployment of Bot Detection Systems:** Implement advanced bot detection tools at key network entry points, such as web application firewalls (WAFs). Configure these systems to analyze traffic patterns and differentiate between human users and bots.

- **Integration with Firewall and IDS:** Connect bot detection tools to our firewall and IDS. Set up automatic rules that block or throttle traffic identified as bot activity. For example, if a bot detection tool flags an IP for repeated suspicious activity, the firewall should immediately limit its access.

- **Endpoint Protection Enhancement:** Ensure that our endpoint protection systems are configured to continuously monitor device behavior. Integrate these systems with our SIEM to provide real-time alerts and automated responses, such as quarantining a device exhibiting signs of compromise.

Behavioral Analysis and Detection

- **Baseline Establishment:** Deploy User and Entity Behavior Analytics (UEBA) tools across our network. Begin by collecting data on user activities, system processes, and network traffic to establish behavioral baselines.

- **Integration with SIEM:** Connect the UEBA tool with our SIEM platform. This allows for real-time data sharing, enabling the SIEM to leverage behavioral insights for more accurate threat detection. For example, if UEBA detects unusual login patterns, this information should be immediately available to the SIEM for further correlation.

- **Automated Response Configuration:** Set up automated workflows within the SIEM to respond to deviations identified by UEBA. This could include actions such as isolating suspicious endpoints, triggering multi-factor authentication for questionable logins, or alerting security teams.

Threat Intelligence Integration

- **Data Feed Configuration:** Begin by setting up secure APIs to connect our Threat Intelligence Platform (TIP) with existing security tools, such as firewalls, IDS, and SIEM systems. Configure these APIs to continuously pull real-time threat data from the TIP.

- **Rule Automation/Control switches:** Use the threat data from the TIP to automatically update firewall and IDS rules. For example, if the TIP identifies a malicious IP, the firewall should block it automatically. Ensure that SIEM systems are

Cybersecurity Redefined: Beyond Traditional Defenses

updated with contextual threat intelligence to enrich event data and improve correlation accuracy.

- **Testing and Validation:** Regularly test the integration by simulating various attack scenarios to ensure that the TIP's intelligence is effectively influencing the behavior of firewalls, IDS, and SIEM systems. Validate that alerts are properly generated and that automated actions, like IP blocking or alert escalation, are functioning as expected.

Deception Technology Integration

- **Honeypot Deployment:** Strategically place honeypots and decoys within our network, focusing on high-value targets or common attack vectors. These should be integrated with our SIEM to ensure that any interaction with these decoys triggers an alert.

- **Automation of Deception Responses:** Configure our SIEM or EDR systems to automatically respond when deception technology is triggered. For example, if an attacker engages with a honeypot, the SIEM should initiate actions such as IP blacklisting, session termination, or additional monitoring.

- **Data Collection and Analysis:** Ensure that all interactions with honeypots and decoys are logged and sent to the SIEM for analysis. Use this data to refine detection algorithms and improve the overall security posture by understanding attacker tactics.

Continuous Monitoring and Cloud-Based Intelligence

- **Cloud Integration:** Connect our endpoint protection systems to cloud-based threat intelligence platforms. Ensure these endpoints receive continuous updates with the latest threat data, enhancing their ability to detect and respond to emerging threats.

- **Real-Time Data Flow:** Establish a real-time data flow between cloud-based intelligence services and on-premise security tools. This allows for the dynamic updating of threat detection models and security policies across the entire infrastructure.

- **Automated Update Processes:** Implement automated processes to ensure that all security tools, including firewalls, IDS, and endpoint protection systems, are regularly updated with the latest threat intelligence. This ensures a unified and current defense posture across the organization.

Testing and Validation

- **End-to-End Testing:** Conduct comprehensive testing to ensure that all integrated systems work together seamlessly. Simulate various attack scenarios to validate that threat intelligence signals, behavioral analysis insights, and automated responses are effectively triggered and managed across the integrated systems.

- **Performance Monitoring:** Continuously monitor the performance of the integrated security systems. Use analytics to assess the effectiveness of the integrations and make adjustments as necessary to optimize the response to threats.

By following these technical integration steps, organizations can ensure that their advanced cybersecurity tools work cohesively with traditional systems, creating a robust and dynamic defense against sophisticated cyber threats.

Key Advantages of Advanced Integration

Enhanced Insider Threat Detection: Traditional methods can sometimes miss insider threats, leaving organizations vulnerable to risks from within. By integrating advanced tools like User and Entity Behavior Analytics (UEBA), organizations gain the ability to continuously monitor user behavior, identifying potential risks early and ensuring that insider threats are detected and mitigated promptly.

Adaptive Access Control Mechanisms: Static access control systems often struggle to detect the misuse of legitimate credentials. Advanced integration enables real-time analysis and adaptive responses, ensuring that any unusual access patterns are quickly identified and addressed, thereby enhancing overall security.

Expanding Security Coverage: While firewalls and Intrusion Detection Systems (IDS) are effective, they have limitations in scope. By incorporating Threat Intelligence Platforms (TIPs), behavioral analysis, bot detection tools, endpoint protection systems, and deception technologies, organizations can significantly extend their security reach, covering gaps that traditional methods may leave exposed.

Precision in Bot Detection and Mitigation: Distinguishing between human users and bots is a challenge for traditional security methods, often leading to breaches. Advanced bot detection tools offer the precision needed to accurately identify and neutralize bot threats, reducing the risk of automated attacks.

Proactive Deception Technology: Traditional security approaches are often reactive, missing opportunities to gather intelligence on attacker methods. Deception technologies, such as honeypots, actively engage attackers, revealing their tactics and providing valuable insights that can be used to strengthen defenses and stay ahead of potential threats.

Conclusion

The integration of advanced cybersecurity tools, as detailed in this chapter, is essential for complementing and enhancing traditional security measures. While traditional tools like firewalls, IDS, and access controls provide a solid foundation, they often fall short in the face of evolving cyber threats. Advanced tools such as User and Entity Behavior Analytics (UEBA), bot detection systems, Threat Intelligence Platforms (TIPs), and deception technologies offer the dynamic, real-time responses necessary to address these gaps.

These advanced tools work in tandem with traditional methods, adding layers of intelligence and adaptability to a security strategy. For instance, while firewalls can block unauthorized access, UEBA can detect insider threats by monitoring behavioral patterns. Similarly, deception technologies go beyond simple detection, actively engaging and revealing attacker tactics that can then be used to strengthen overall defenses.

In conclusion, the synergy between advanced cybersecurity tools and traditional methods creates a more comprehensive and effective defense against modern cyber threats. By integrating these tools, organizations can better protect their digital assets, respond to threats in real-time, and maintain a robust security posture in an increasingly complex digital landscape.

References:

https://www.f5.com/resources/solution-guides/bot-detection-and-security

https://chargebacks911.com/fraud-detection/

https://www.arkoselabs.com/anti-bot/bot-detection/

https://seon.io/resources/bot-attacks/

https://fingerprint.com/blog/build-our-own-bot-detection-script/

https://www.oracle.com/artificial-intelligence/ai-model-training/

https://landing.ai/blog/model-training-with-machine-learning

https://humansignal.com/blog/guide-building-a-data-labeling-practice-for-machine-learning-and-data-science/

https://scale.com/guides/data-labeling-annotation-guide

https://www.cisco.com/c/en/us/products/security/endpoint-security/index.html

https://www.imperva.com/learn/data-security/ueba-user-and-entity-behavior-analytics/

https://www.rapid7.com/fundamentals/deception-technology/

https://www.checkpoint.com/cyber-hub/cyber-security/what-is-a-threat-intelligence-platform-tip/#ThreatIntelligencePlatforms

https://www.rapid7.com/fundamentals/honeypots/

https://www.bluevoyant.com/knowledge-center/threat-intelligence-complete-guide-to-process-and-technology

https://threatconnect.com/threat-intelligence-platform/

4

Scaling Security: Building Reliable Threat Detection Systems

In today's digital landscape, where cyber threats are growing in sophistication and frequency, the scalability and reliability of cybersecurity tools have become critical. Tools such as bot detection systems and behavioral analysis platforms are essential for safeguarding organizations, but their effectiveness depends heavily on the infrastructure supporting them. Advanced algorithms and detection methods can only perform as intended if the systems running them can handle the demands of high traffic volumes and complex data analysis. Without adequate scalability, these tools may become overwhelmed during peak usage, leading to gaps in security coverage.

However, scalability must be balanced with cost efficiency. Over-provisioning resources can drive up costs, potentially undermining the business model. The challenge lies in designing systems that can dynamically scale to meet demand without incurring unnecessary expenses. This chapter will explore the technical challenges and solutions for building scalable and reliable cybersecurity tools. By understanding how to optimize infrastructure, organizations can ensure their security measures remain robust, efficient, and cost-effective, even under the most demanding conditions.

Scalability in Security Tooling

Scalability is essential for advanced security tools like bot detection and behavioral analysis, which must handle increasing data volumes and complex threats without losing performance. Effective scalability involves more than just adding resources; it requires strategic planning to distribute workloads, optimize resource use, and ensure high availability. This chapter outlines strategies to build scalable, reliable security systems that can adapt to evolving cyber threats while remaining cost-effective and resilient.

Growing User Base: As organizations expand, the number of users interacting with systems increases. For security tools, this means more data points to analyze and more traffic to monitor. For instance, a bot detection system must efficiently scale to handle spikes in user activity without slowing down, especially during events like sales or product launches.

Expanding Feature Set: Security tools often need to evolve, adding new features or integrating with other systems to improve effectiveness. For example, integrating a behavioral analysis tool with additional data sources like mobile devices or IoT networks adds complexity but also enhances detection capabilities. Scalability ensures that these enhancements do not degrade performance.

Increasing Data Volume: Over time, the amount of data that security tools must process grows exponentially. For bot detection and behavioral analysis, this data could include user interactions, network traffic logs, and more. Scalability in data processing capabilities is essential to maintain quick and accurate threat detection as the data volume increases.

Complexity in Infrastructure: As security infrastructures grow, the connections between systems become more complex. For instance, as a bot detection tool integrates with more parts of a network—such as APIs, third-party services, and cloud environments—the system's overall complexity increases. Scalability helps manage this complexity, ensuring that each component can communicate effectively without bottlenecks.

Geographical Expansion: When an organization expands into new regions or countries, the security tools must scale to protect a broader and more diverse user base. This might involve adapting bot detection algorithms to different traffic patterns or ensuring that behavioral analysis tools are effective across varied cultural contexts.

In summary, scalability is not just about handling more; it's about handling more efficiently and effectively. For security tools, this means ensuring that as our systems grow in size, complexity, and geographical reach, they continue to provide robust protection against evolving cyber threats without incurring prohibitive costs or sacrificing performance.

Scalability Metrics: Essential Focus Areas

Scalability is a critical aspect of system design, especially for advanced security tools like bot detection and behavior analysis. To ensure that these tools can handle growing demands without compromising performance, it is essential to measure and optimize their scalability. Inefficient scalability can lead to degraded performance, increased latency, and higher operational costs, which can ultimately undermine the effectiveness of our cybersecurity measures.

Performance Metrics

Response Time and Latency: This measures how quickly a system responds to requests under varying loads. In the context of cybersecurity tools, low latency is crucial for real-time threat detection and response. For example, during a surge in network traffic due to a DDoS attack, a scalable system should maintain low response times to ensure timely identification and mitigation of threats.

Throughput: This metric assesses the system's capacity to process a high volume of transactions or data within a specific timeframe. High throughput is essential for tools like behavior analysis, which must process large datasets to detect anomalies without causing bottlenecks. A well-designed scalable system can increase throughput as data volume grows, ensuring continuous monitoring and protection.

Elasticity Metrics

Auto-Scaling Accuracy: Elasticity refers to a system's ability to automatically scale resources up or down based on demand. Accurate auto-scaling ensures that our security tools have enough resources during peak loads, such as during a cyberattack, but do not over-provision resources during normal operations, which can lead to unnecessary costs.

Resource Utilization Ratios: Efficient resource utilization is key to balancing performance with cost. For instance, a bot detection system that scales out by deploying additional instances during peak traffic should also scale back down during off-peak periods to optimize resource use and control costs.

Resilience Metrics

Mean Time Between Failures (MTBF): This measures the average time between system failures, indicating the reliability of the system under increased load. For security tools, a high MTBF ensures continuous protection even as demands increase, preventing downtime during critical periods.

Mean Time to Recovery (MTTR): This metric tracks the time it takes to recover from a failure. In a scalable security infrastructure, quick recovery times are essential to minimize the impact of failures, ensuring that systems can swiftly return to normal operation after an issue.

Best Practices to keep System Performance in check

To effectively measure and ensure scalability, industry standards and best practices provide guidance:

Service Level Agreements (SLAs): Define performance benchmarks that security tools must meet, such as response times under specific load conditions. These SLAs ensure that scalability metrics are aligned with organizational goals.

Load Testing and Stress Testing: Regularly perform load and stress tests to evaluate how security tools perform under varying levels of demand. Tools like Apache JMeter or Gatling can simulate high-traffic scenarios to assess system behavior, helping identify potential scalability bottlenecks before they impact real-world operations.

Capacity Planning: Anticipate future growth in user base, data volume, and threat landscape. Capacity planning helps ensure that our security infrastructure can scale efficiently without over-provisioning, which can lead to inflated costs.

Balancing Scalability with Cost: While it's crucial to design systems that can scale effectively, it's equally important to manage costs. Over-provisioning resources can lead to excessive expenses, defeating the business model's purpose. To strike the right balance:

Dynamic Scaling: Implement dynamic scaling policies that adjust resources in real-time based on demand, rather than relying on static provisioning. This approach ensures that resources are allocated efficiently, reducing unnecessary costs.

Cost Monitoring Tools: Use cost monitoring and optimization tools to track resource usage and expenditures. For example, AWS Cost Explorer or Azure Cost Management can provide insights into where resources are being over-utilized or under-utilized, enabling more precise adjustments.

Measuring and optimizing the scalability of advanced security tools is essential for maintaining robust and reliable protection in an increasingly complex digital environment. By focusing on key scalability metrics, adhering to industry standards, and balancing performance with cost, organizations can ensure that their cybersecurity infrastructure is both efficient and effective.

Key Takeaways

	Handle Increased Traffic	Ensures the system can manage growing user demands without degrading performance.
	Support Data Growth	Accommodates expanding data volumes without compromising efficiency.
	Response Time	Measures how quickly the system responds under increased load.
	Throughput	Assesses the volume of data processed by the system in a given time.
	Resource Utilization	Evaluates how efficiently system resources are used during scaling.
	Latency	Tracks delays in processing and communication as load increases.
	Capacity	Determines the maximum load the system can handle before performance declines.

How to Achieve Scalability

Achieving scalability requires a multifaceted approach that balances cost-effectiveness, performance, and fault tolerance. Here are some common techniques to achieve scalability.

Scaling Security: Building Reliable Threat Detection Systems

Vertical Scaling (Scale-Up): Vertical scaling involves increasing the capacity of existing hardware, such as adding more RAM, faster CPUs, or additional storage to a server. This method is straightforward and can effectively boost performance in a single instance of a security tool. For example, a behavior analysis tool might need additional processing power to handle more complex machine learning algorithms as traffic grows.

However, vertical scaling has limitations. There's a ceiling to how much we can scale a single server, and it introduces a single point of failure. If the server crashes, the entire security tool goes down, leaving the system vulnerable. Additionally, while scaling up can enhance capacity, it often comes with increased costs, which can impact the overall business model.

Horizontal Scaling (Scale-Out): Horizontal scaling is more flexible and involves adding more servers to distribute the workload. This method is particularly useful for tools like bot detection, where the workload can be spread across multiple servers to analyze different segments of incoming traffic simultaneously. For example, if an organization experiences a surge in traffic due to a DDoS attack, horizontally scaling the bot detection tool across multiple servers can help manage the load effectively. This method also enhances fault tolerance, as the failure of one server doesn't bring down the entire system. However, horizontal scaling introduces complexity in managing distributed systems and requires effective load balancing to ensure that each server shares the workload evenly.

Auto-Scaling: Auto-scaling automatically adjusts the number of active servers based on the current load. This feature is especially useful for security tools that experience fluctuating traffic. For example, if bot traffic spikes during a particular time of day, auto-scaling can bring more servers online to handle the increased load, then scale back down when traffic decreases. Auto-scaling ensures that the system remains responsive under varying loads without requiring manual intervention, making it a critical feature for maintaining performance and cost efficiency.

Time-Based Scaling: Analyze historical data to determine when our security tools (like bot detection and behavioral analysis systems) experience the highest demand. For instance, e-commerce sites may experience peaks during holiday seasons or flash sales. Configure scaling policies to automatically add resources before anticipated peak times and reduce them during off-peak hours. For example, schedule increased server capacity during the day when user activity is highest and scale down at night.

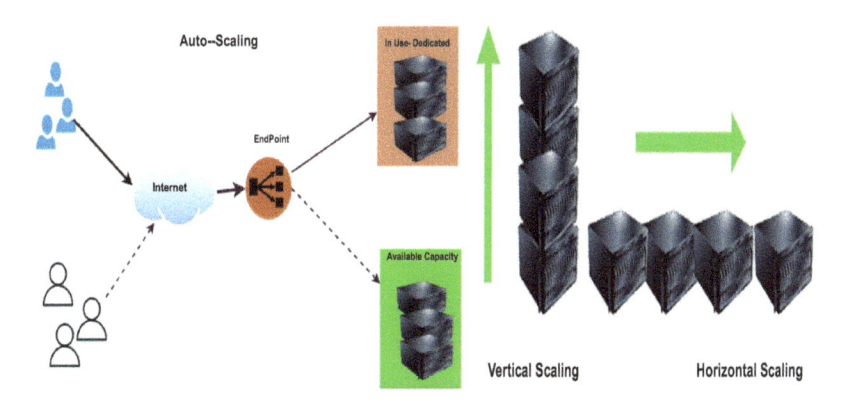

Regularly monitor and adjust time-based scaling to ensure it meets demand, and consider combining it with demand-based scaling for more responsive and effective resource management.

Scaling Security: Building Reliable Threat Detection Systems

Load Balancing: Load balancing is crucial for both vertical and horizontal scaling. It involves distributing incoming traffic across multiple servers to prevent any single server from becoming overwhelmed. In the context of security tools, load balancing ensures that traffic is evenly distributed, allowing tools like bot detection and behavior analysis to function optimally without delays or performance drops.

For instance, during a high-traffic event, a load balancer can direct traffic to the least busy server, ensuring that all servers work efficiently without overloading any one server. This improves the overall reliability and responsiveness of the security system.

Asynchronous Processing: For tasks that are not time-sensitive or require heavy computation, asynchronous processing can offload these tasks to background processes. In the context of behavior analysis, tasks such as in-depth user profiling can be handled asynchronously, allowing real-time analysis to continue uninterrupted.

By deferring these tasks, the system can focus on immediate threat detection and response, improving overall efficiency without compromising on thoroughness.

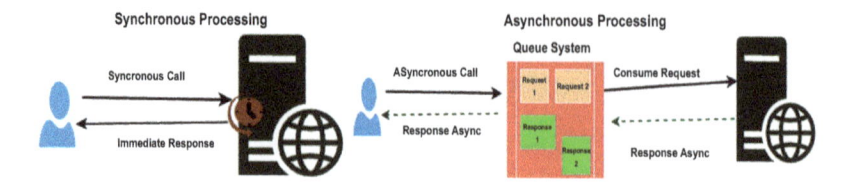

Partitioning: Partitioning is a fundamental strategy in scaling systems, particularly when dealing with large datasets or high-traffic applications. By splitting data or functionality across multiple nodes or servers, partitioning distributes the workload, which helps in avoiding bottlenecks that can slow down system performance.

- **Data Partitioning:** Involves dividing a large dataset into smaller, more manageable pieces. These partitions can be based on various factors such as user ID, geographic region, or any other logical division that makes sense for the application. Each partition is then stored on a different server or node, allowing the system to process queries and operations more efficiently by working on smaller subsets of data.

- **Functional Partitioning:** Separates different functionalities of an application across multiple servers. For example, in a security tool like bot detection, one server could handle real-time traffic analysis while another manages user behavior tracking. This ensures that no single server becomes a bottleneck, thus improving overall system performance and reliability.

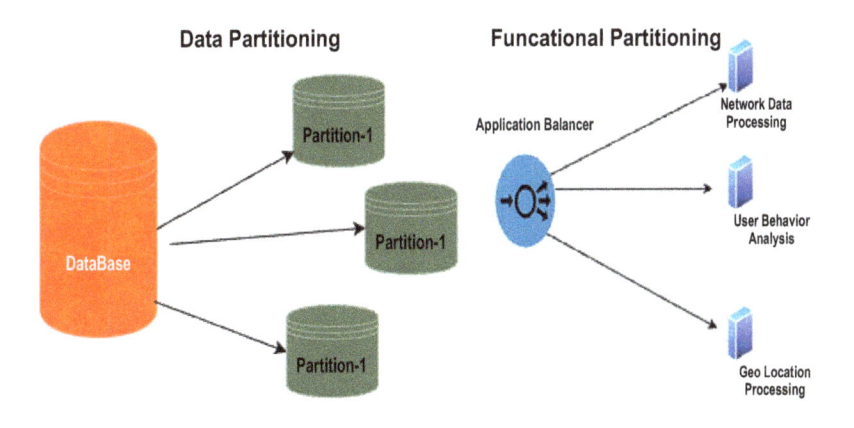

Scaling Security: Building Reliable Threat Detection Systems

Example: In a bot detection system, partitioning can be used to allocate different parts of the dataset (e.g., logs from different regions) to different servers. This way, the system can handle large volumes of data simultaneously without overwhelming a single server.

Multi-Region Deployment: Multi-region deployment involves distributing applications and services across multiple geographic locations or cloud regions. This strategy significantly enhances scalability, reduces latency, and improves redundancy. It is essential for global applications requiring high availability and compliance with local regulations.Key Benefits as follow:

Enhanced Scalability By processing and analyzing data locally in different regions, multi-region deployment reduces server load and improves the system's capacity to handle large-scale operations, such as during widespread cyberattacks.

Improved Redundancy If one region's data center fails or is compromised, others can continue to operate, ensuring uninterrupted security operations.

Reduced Latency Placing data and processing closer to users minimizes delays, leading to faster response times and better performance.

Compliance with Local Regulations Storing sensitive data within specific geographic boundaries helps meet regional legal requirements, such as GDPR in the European Union.

Multi-region deployment is a powerful strategy for creating scalable, resilient, and compliant security applications, enabling robust global threat management while maintaining high performance.

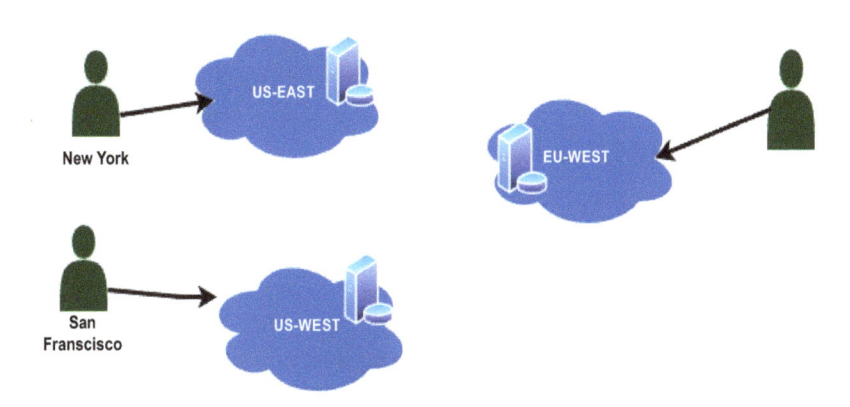

Example: A behavior analysis tool might be deployed across multiple regions to ensure that data from users in different parts of the world is processed with minimal delay. This setup not only improves the user experience but also ensures that the system remains responsive even under high traffic conditions.

Challenges and Trade-offs for Scalability

Balancing Cost and Scalability: Scaling systems often comes with increased costs, such as additional servers and infrastructure. It's crucial to weigh these costs against the performance and reliability gains to ensure efficient resource use.

Consistency vs. Availability: In distributed systems, ensuring data consistency can sometimes reduce availability. Finding the right balance between these two is critical to maintaining both performance and reliability.

Latency vs. Throughput: Optimizing for low latency may reduce overall throughput, and vice versa. Striking a balance between these factors is key to maintaining a responsive and efficient system.

Scaling Security: Building Reliable Threat Detection Systems

Effective Data Partitioning: Proper data partitioning improves scalability by distributing workloads evenly, but poor partitioning can lead to system imbalances, where some nodes are overburdened while others are underutilized. Careful planning is required to avoid these issues.

Key Takeaways

	Load Balancing	Balances incoming traffic across multiple servers to prevent overload on any single server.
	Horizontal Scaling	Add servers or nodes to increase capacity without major architectural changes.
	Vertical Scaling	Upgrading existing server resources, like CPU or memory, to handle more load within the same physical machine.
	Database Sharding	Splits large databases into smaller, more manageable pieces (shards), each hosted on a different server.
	Auto-scaling	Dynamically adjusts the number of active servers or resources based on current traffic or load, optimizing cost and performance

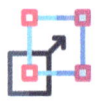

Enhancing Reliability in Cybersecurity Tools

In the fast-evolving landscape of cybersecurity, ensuring the reliability of our security tools is as critical as scalability. As mentioned earlier in this chapter, scalability enables our system to handle increased traffic and threats without compromising performance. However, reliability focuses on maintaining consistent protection and operational efficiency, even under pressure. Both scalability and reliability are essential to safeguarding our systems against evolving threats while supporting business growth.

The Dual Nature of Reliability: Availability and Accuracy

Reliability in cybersecurity is a multifaceted concept that encompasses both the availability of the system and the accuracy of its responses. While uptime ensures that the system remains operational, it is equally crucial that the system responds promptly and accurately to potential threats. High traffic volumes and unexpected surges can challenge both these aspects, making it essential to maintain a balance. A system that is online but fails to detect or respond to a security threat is not truly reliable. Therefore, the reliability of cybersecurity tools must be measured by their ability to remain available and deliver precise threat detection and response under all conditions.

Key Metrics for Ensuring Cybersecurity Reliability

To maintain and enhance the reliability of cybersecurity systems, it's crucial to monitor key performance indicators (KPIs) that directly impact system performance and resilience. These metrics provide essential insights into how well a system can protect against threats and maintain consistent operation.

Threat Response Time: Measuring how quickly a system detects and mitigates threats is vital. The faster a system can respond, the more effectively it can minimize damage during cyberattacks. For instance, in the event of a ransomware attack, a quick response can isolate affected systems before the malware spreads, thereby preventing widespread data loss.

Accuracy of Threat Detection: The accuracy of a system in distinguishing real threats from benign activities is measured by the false positive/negative rate. A high false positive rate can lead to unnecessary alerts, causing alert fatigue and potentially resulting in overlooked real threats. Conversely, a high false negative rate means that actual threats might go undetected, posing serious security risks. For example, an intrusion detection system (IDS) might incorrectly flag normal user behavior as suspicious (false positive) or fail to detect a covert attack (false negative), affecting overall security operations.

System Performance (Data Throughput and Uptime): Data throughput refers to the system's ability to handle increased traffic without performance degradation. This is particularly critical during high-demand periods, such as Distributed Denial of Service (DDoS) attacks, where maintaining high throughput ensures that the system remains functional and secure. For example, during Black Friday, e-commerce sites rely on high data throughput to manage traffic surges while preventing slowdowns that could be exploited by attackers.

Uptime, on the other hand, indicates the percentage of time the system is operational. A system designed for high uptime, such as 99.999%, experiences minimal downtime, which is crucial for continuous protection against threats. Financial institutions, for instance, aim for near-perfect uptime to ensure continuous transaction processing and prevent vulnerabilities during maintenance or downtime.

System Reliability (Failure Metrics and Fault Tolerance): Failure rate, mean time between failures (MTBF), and mean time to repair (MTTR) are critical metrics that gauge system stability, robustness, and recovery efficiency. A low failure rate and a high MTBF indicate a reliable system, while a short MTTR reflects efficient recovery processes. Additionally, fault tolerance is essential for ensuring that the system continues operating during a failure. In a distributed security architecture, for example, if one node fails, others can take over the workload, preventing service disruption and maintaining security.

Resource Utilization (Saturation): Monitoring resource utilization, or saturation, is key to preventing systems from becoming overwhelmed. During high-traffic security scenarios, such as DDoS attacks, managing saturation through load balancing and scaling strategies helps distribute traffic evenly, ensuring the system remains operational even under intense pressure.

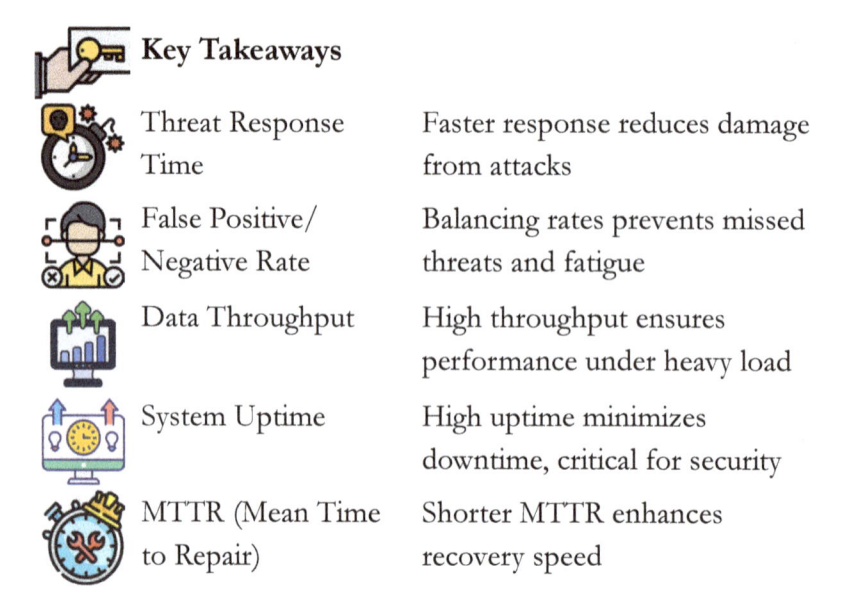

Key Takeaways

	Threat Response Time	Faster response reduces damage from attacks
	False Positive/Negative Rate	Balancing rates prevents missed threats and fatigue
	Data Throughput	High throughput ensures performance under heavy load
	System Uptime	High uptime minimizes downtime, critical for security
	MTTR (Mean Time to Repair)	Shorter MTTR enhances recovery speed

Building a robust cybersecurity defense requires both high availability and precise threat detection. Aiming for 99.99% uptime and using predictive analytics can enhance reliability by anticipating issues. Balancing uptime with accurate detection ensures resilient systems capable of countering sophisticated attacks. By monitoring key metrics, organizations can keep their security tools reliable and effective, even in challenging conditions. This section outlines essential metrics and strategies to maintain and improve the performance of security tools under pressure.

Monitoring and Observability: Strengthening Cybersecurity

Achieving high reliability in security systems requires a comprehensive approach that combines multiple strategies to ensure robustness and resilience. Monitoring tracks system health and performance, while observability provides deeper insights to understand and resolve underlying issues effectively.

Monitoring involves the collection of data from IT resources to track their status and performance. It helps in identifying when and where a problem exists, serving as the first line of defense in system management.

Observability takes a more advanced approach by combining data from multiple sources to gain actionable insights into system behavior. It doesn't just indicate what is wrong, but also why it's happening, offering the context necessary for effective problem-solving.

Metrics for Monitoring and Observability

In today's cybersecurity landscape, monitoring and observability are crucial for maintaining system reliability. Monitoring provides vital data on performance and health, while observability digs deeper, offering insights into the root causes of issues and how to resolve them. Together, these practices are the cornerstone of building and sustaining resilient, high-performing systems capable of handling complex challenges.

To ensure our security tools and systems remain reliable, focus on the following essential metrics:

System Performance

- **CPU and Memory Usage** Monitor resource consumption to avoid overload and identify potential bottlenecks.

- **Request Latency and Response** Time Measure how quickly our systems respond to requests, which is critical for maintaining user experience.

- **Throughput** Track the rate at which data is processed to ensure efficiency and detect any slowdowns.

Infrastructure Health

- **Server Health and Disk Space** Ensure optimal server performance and sufficient storage to prevent system failures.

- **Network Bandwidth and CPU Temperature** Monitor these metrics to prevent network congestion and avoid hardware damage due to overheating.

Application Performance

- **Active Users and Request Volume** Gauge the load on applications to scale resources appropriately.

- **Error Rate** Identify and troubleshoot frequent errors to enhance application stability.

Monitoring and Observability in Action

Robust monitoring and observability is crucial for ensuring the reliability and performance of security tools. Grafana and Sensu are two powerful platforms that, when combined, provide a comprehensive solution for managing complex, dynamic IT environments.

Grafana: Visualizing and Analyzing System Performance

Grafana is a leading tool for monitoring and observability, offering rich, customizable dashboards that integrate data from various sources. It excels in visualizing system performance metrics, enabling teams to monitor real-time data across multiple environments.

Comprehensive Dashboards Grafana's dashboards aggregate data from multiple sources, such as Prometheus, SQL databases, and JSON APIs, presenting it in intuitive visual formats. This capability allows security teams to quickly identify and troubleshoot issues, optimizing the performance and reliability of their tools.

Advanced Querying Grafana supports a wide range of query languages and data transformations, enabling precise analysis of security metrics. This flexibility is crucial for addressing specific monitoring needs and enhancing system insights.

Application Observability Grafana provides detailed visibility into application and frontend performance, minimizing the mean time to repair (MTTR) for incidents by leveraging OpenTelemetry and Prometheus data models.

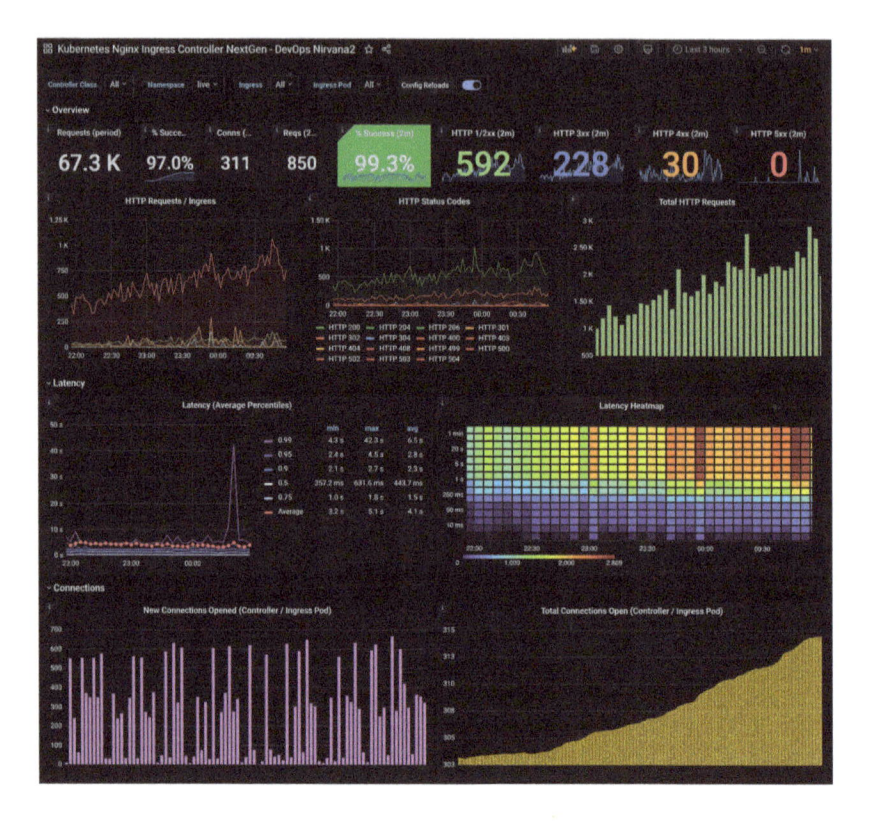

Image credit: https://grafana.com/media/docs/grafana/dashboards-overview/complex-dashboard-example.png

Sensu: Automating and Scaling Monitoring Workflows

Sensu complements Grafana by offering a robust platform for automating and scaling monitoring workflows. It is designed to handle the complexities of cloud-native and containerized environments, making it a key tool for maintaining system reliability.

Beyond Firewalls: *Security at Scale*

Monitoring-as-Code Sensu enables teams to manage monitoring configurations as code, automating the deployment and scaling of monitoring in dynamic environments. This approach ensures that monitoring remains consistent and up-to-date, even as infrastructure evolves.

Automated Incident Response Sensu's event-driven architecture supports automated incident responses, such as service restarts or triggering custom scripts, reducing the need for manual intervention and improving response times.

Unified Observability Pipeline Sensu consolidates monitoring across different environments and tools, eliminating data silos and providing a single, cohesive observability pipeline. It integrates seamlessly with tools like Grafana, Prometheus, and Nagios, allowing for comprehensive monitoring across all layers of the infrastructure.

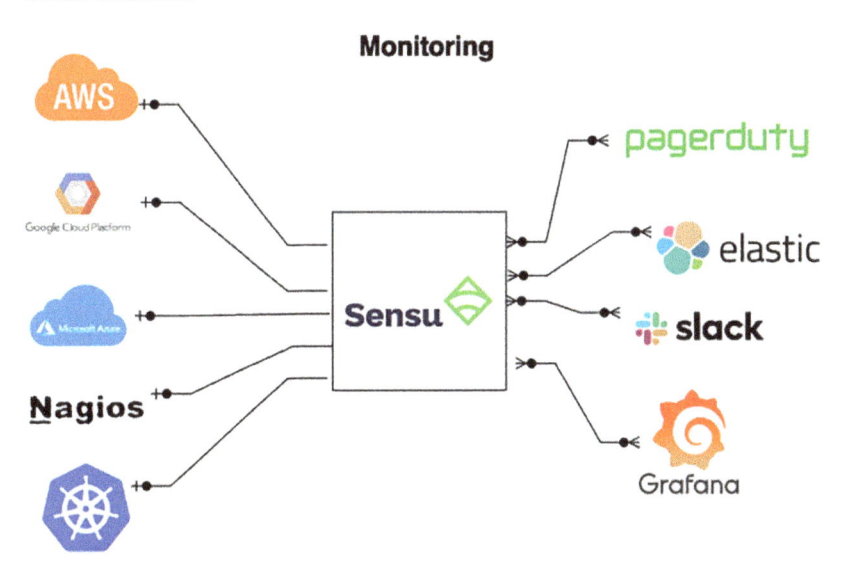

Implementing monitoring and observability with Grafana and Sensu equips organizations with the tools needed to manage complex IT environments effectively. By leveraging Grafana's powerful visualization capabilities and Sensu's robust automation and scaling features, security teams can ensure their systems remain resilient, responsive, and secure in the face of evolving challenges.

Tracing and Logging: Digging Deeper

Beyond basic metrics, traces and logs offer a detailed view of system operations, especially in complex, distributed environments

Tracing

- **HTTP Requests and Database Queries** Trace the flow of requests to pinpoint where delays or failures occur, helping to optimize performance.

- **RPC and Function Calls** Monitor service interactions to troubleshoot communication issues and enhance function performance.

Logging

- **System and Error Logs** These logs help track system events and identify runtime errors, essential for debugging and maintaining system health.

- **Security and Audit Logs** Use these logs to detect security breaches and ensure compliance by maintaining detailed records of system activities.

Log information offers a comprehensive view of system activities, enabling quick identification of issues like DoS attacks by analyzing access logs to trace the source. For instance, if an application feature triggers high error rates, log analysis can pinpoint the problematic parameter for immediate correction. Using the ELK stack (Elasticsearch, Logstash, Kibana) streamlines this process, with Filebeat shipping logs to Logstash for parsing, Elasticsearch for storage, and Kibana for visualizing and analyzing the data.

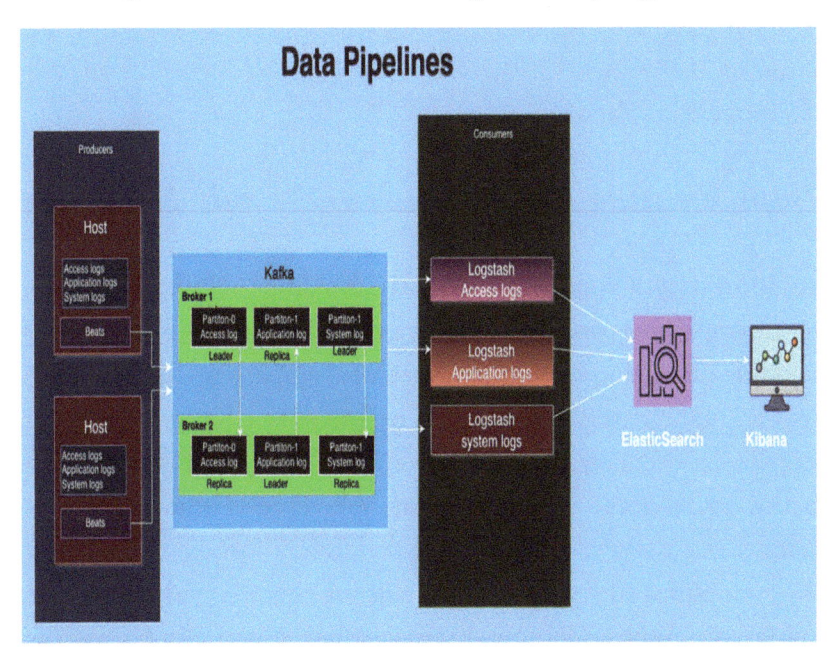

Observability goes beyond traditional monitoring by providing the necessary context and insights for maintaining system reliability. It enables teams to understand not just what went wrong, but why, allowing for precise root cause analysis and faster issue resolution. By implementing centralized logging, comprehensive tracing, and automated alerts, organizations can enhance their monitoring efforts and ensure that their security tools remain robust and adaptable.

Scaling Security: Building Reliable Threat Detection Systems

Measuring the impact of these practices through key metrics like incident frequency, rollback rates, and MTTR helps track improvements in reliability. Ultimately, in the fast-paced world of cybersecurity, monitoring and observability are indispensable for maintaining the uptime, performance, and resilience of complex systems. They are the backbone of a reliable cybersecurity strategy, ensuring that systems can quickly adapt to and recover from any challenges they face.

Implementing Redundancy and Fault Tolerance

Redundancy involves creating backup components or pathways to ensure that if one part of a system fails, others can take over without disrupting service. For instance, global systems often use multiple data centers spread across regions so that if one center goes offline, another can seamlessly maintain operations. Similarly, load balancers distribute traffic across multiple servers and automatically reroute it if a server fails, ensuring continuous uptime. AWS Route 53 exemplifies this by providing failover routing, which redirects traffic to healthy endpoints during outages, further illustrating the importance of redundancy in maintaining service continuity.

Fault tolerance refers to a system's ability to continue operating properly even when some components fail. For example, Kafka and Elasticsearch use data partitioning and leader replicas to ensure that if a leader replica fails, a follower is automatically promoted, keeping the system operational. In cloud-based environments, fault tolerance is also demonstrated through automatic failover mechanisms, where traffic is redirected to a secondary server if the primary one fails, ensuring users experience no disruption in service. This ability to handle failures gracefully is key to maintaining system reliability and performance.

Retrying Mechanisms and Circuit Breakers

Retries and circuit breakers are essential strategies for maintaining system stability, especially in complex, high-traffic environments.

Retry Mechanisms When a security request fails due to transient issues, such as temporary network outages or brief server overloads, implementing a retry mechanism allows the system to automatically retry the operation. This approach helps recover from minor disruptions without overwhelming network or backend services. For instance, if a request to an authentication server times out, the system can automatically retry after a brief delay, improving the chances of successful processing without causing additional strain.

Circuit Breakers For more persistent errors, deploying circuit breakers prevents repeated attempts that could further burden the system. A circuit breaker monitors the success and failure rates of operations; when failures exceed a certain threshold, the circuit breaker "trips" and stops further retries, preventing additional load on already stressed components. For example, Elasticsearch uses a circuit breaker mechanism to protect the system from overwhelming memory usage by halting further operations when a memory threshold is reached, thus safeguarding system stability. Similarly, during a DDoS attack, a circuit breaker can stop excessive retries that could exacerbate the attack's impact.

Retry and Circuit Breaker in Action

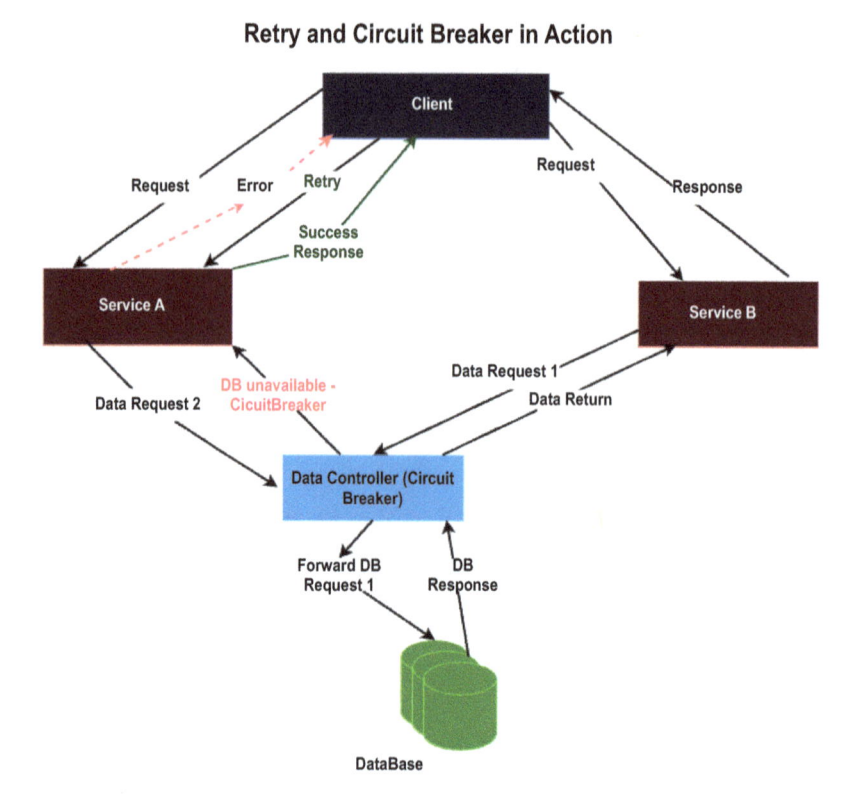

Conclusion

Building reliable security systems is not just about preventing downtime; it's about ensuring systems can withstand and recover from inevitable challenges. This requires a careful balance between cost and performance, focusing investments where they have the most impact, such as critical systems and peak traffic periods. Implementing load-balancing, auto-scaling, and other strategies like redundancy, retries, and continuous monitoring ensures that our systems remain resilient, even in the face of adversity.

Beyond Firewalls: *Security at Scale*

As digital threats become more complex, scalability and reliability are essential. Strategies like data replication and caching play a critical role in keeping security systems robust under stress. Reliability means more than just staying online—it's about ensuring systems function correctly, tolerate errors, and recover smoothly from failures.

Ultimately, building scalable and reliable cybersecurity tools is a challenging but essential task. The principles discussed in this chapter provide a strong foundation for developing systems that can meet the demands of today's digital landscape, ensuring both performance and security are maintained without compromise.

Key Takeaways

	Redundancy	Use backup systems and data centers to ensure continuous operation.
	Fault Tolerance	Design systems to handle failures gracefully without service disruption.
	Retry Mechanisms	Automatically retry failed requests to recover from transient errors.
	Circuit Breakers	Prevent repeated failures by halting retries after a certain threshold.
	Observability	Gain deep insights into system behavior to understand and resolve issues.

Scaling Security: Building Reliable Threat Detection Systems

Reference:

https://www.flagright.com/post/how-to-scale-our-fraud-prevention-systems

https://flinthillsgroup.com/10-essential-tips-for-building-a-scalable-cybersecurity-solution/

https://www.educative.io/blog/scalable-systems-101

https://madappgang.com/blog/scalability-in-cybersecurity-development/

https://www.markovml.com/blog/model-scalability

https://medium.com/@amirsina.torfi/scalability-in-machine-learning-systems-challenges-strategies-and-best-practices-231cc2fb2889

https://medium.com/oolooroo/crafting-scalable-systems-practices-patterns-and-principles-7b6b7b95c4ed

https://grafana.com/docs/grafana-cloud/introduction/dashboards/

https://linkedin.github.io/school-of-sre/level101/metrics_and_monitoring/observability/

5

Data at the Core: Ensuring Availability, Localization, and Security

In the rapidly evolving landscape of cybersecurity, the ability to process, protect, and access vast amounts of data efficiently is critical. Security tools operate on complex and massive datasets that require high-performance data pipelines to ensure real-time threat detection and analysis. This chapter delves into the essential strategies for optimizing data availability, enhancing protection measures, and improving accessibility to build resilient and scalable security applications.

A basic representation of a data platform.

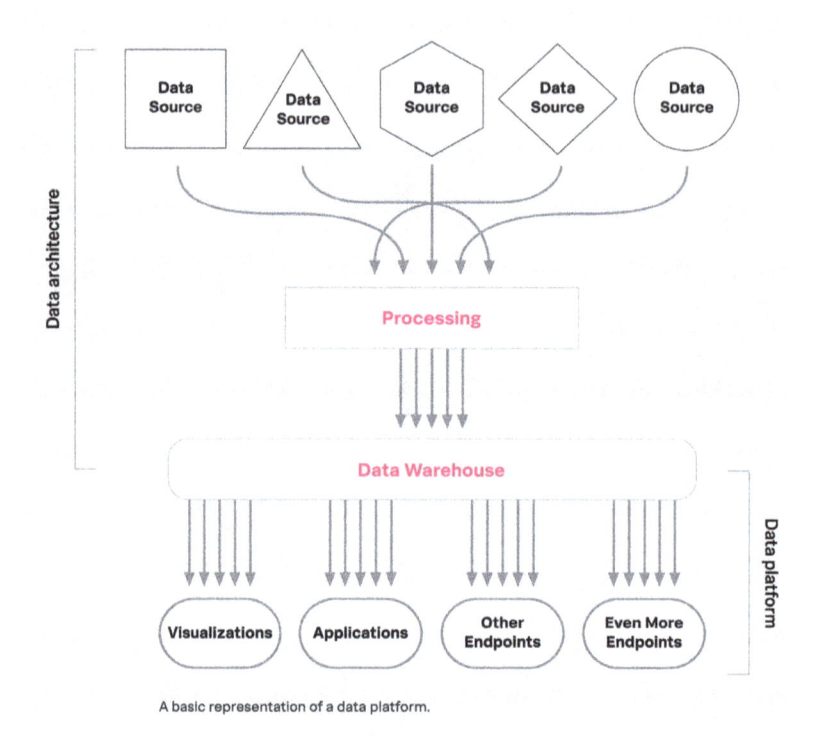

Image Credit: https://www.splunk.com/content/dam/splunk2/images/data-insider/data-platform/data-platform-1.svg

Data Pipelines for Enhanced Security

A data pipeline is a series of processes designed to collect, transform, and store data, making it ready for analysis. In the context of security tools, data pipelines are essential for processing vast amounts of data from various sources to identify patterns, detect anomalies, and prevent fraud. These pipelines move data from applications, network logs, IoT devices, and other digital

Beyond Firewalls: *Security at Scale*

channels to a central location where it is cleaned, optimized, and organized for security analysis.

Benefits of a Data Pipeline in Security Tools

Improved Data Quality: Pipelines clean and standardize data, ensuring accuracy and consistency across security tools, which is crucial for identifying patterns and anomalies in cybersecurity.

Efficient Data Processing: Automation of data transformation allows security engineers to focus on detecting threats rather than manual data handling, speeding up the identification of security incidents.

Comprehensive Data Integration: Data pipelines merge and reconcile data from multiple sources, resolving inconsistencies and enhancing the reliability of security analyses. For example, correcting minor discrepancies in user data across platforms ensures accurate tracking of suspicious activities.

Cost and Time Efficiency: By processing only relevant data, pipelines reduce unnecessary reprocessing, saving resources and enabling faster response to potential threats.

Real-Time Analysis: Pipelines enable continuous data flow, allowing for real-time updates and immediate detection of security breaches, which is vital for proactive threat management.

Techniques for Optimizing Data Pipelines in Security Tools

Optimized Data Formats: Utilizing optimized data formats such as Apache Parquet improves query performance by allowing faster access to specific data points without needing to scan entire datasets. For example, a security tool might store network logs in Parquet format, which enables quick filtering and retrieval of specific IP addresses or timestamps during an investigation, significantly reducing the time required for threat detection and response.

In-Memory Data Processing: In-memory processing stores critical data in RAM, which drastically reduces latency and enables rapid data retrieval. For instance, Redis can be used to store frequently accessed threat signatures in memory, allowing a security tool to instantly compare incoming data against known threats. This approach is especially effective in scenarios like DDoS attacks, where quick data processing is crucial.

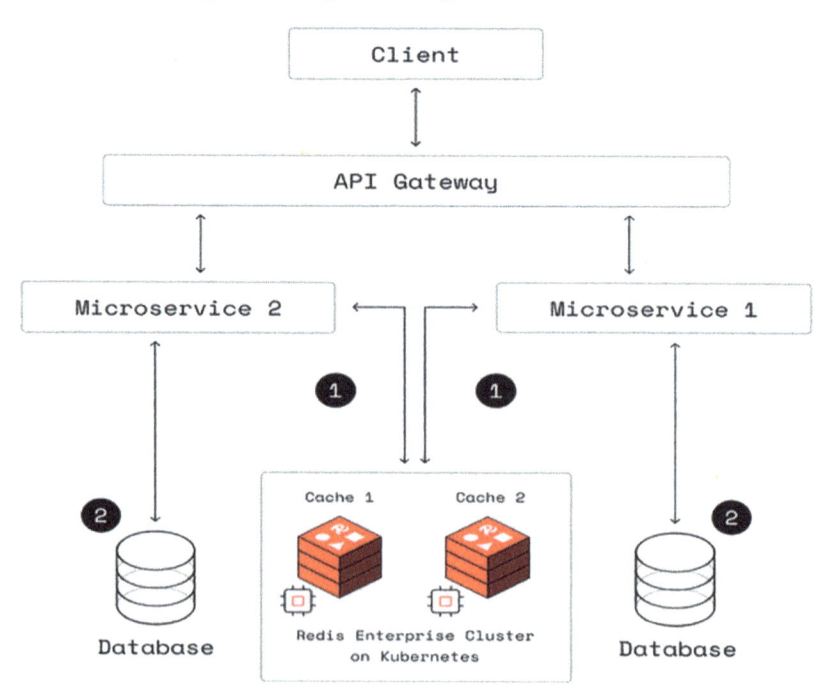

Image credit : *https://redis.io/solutions/caching/*

Beyond Firewalls: *Security at Scale*

Sharding and Replication: Sharding divides large datasets across multiple databases or servers, reducing load and improving performance, while replication ensures data is duplicated across multiple locations for enhanced availability and fault tolerance. For example, Kafka can shard streaming data across different partitions, ensuring efficient processing, while Elasticsearch replicates indexes across multiple nodes, maintaining search capabilities even if some nodes fail.

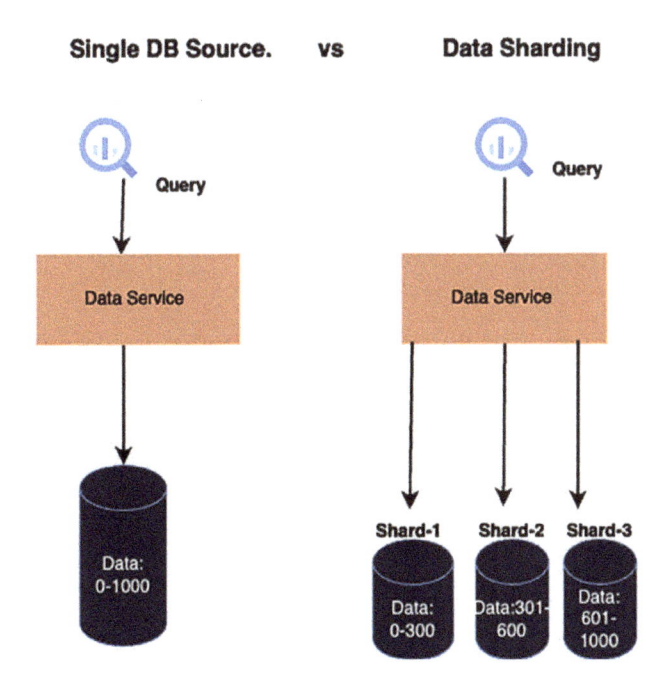

Data at the Core: Ensuring Availability, Localization, and Security

Data Replication with Sharding

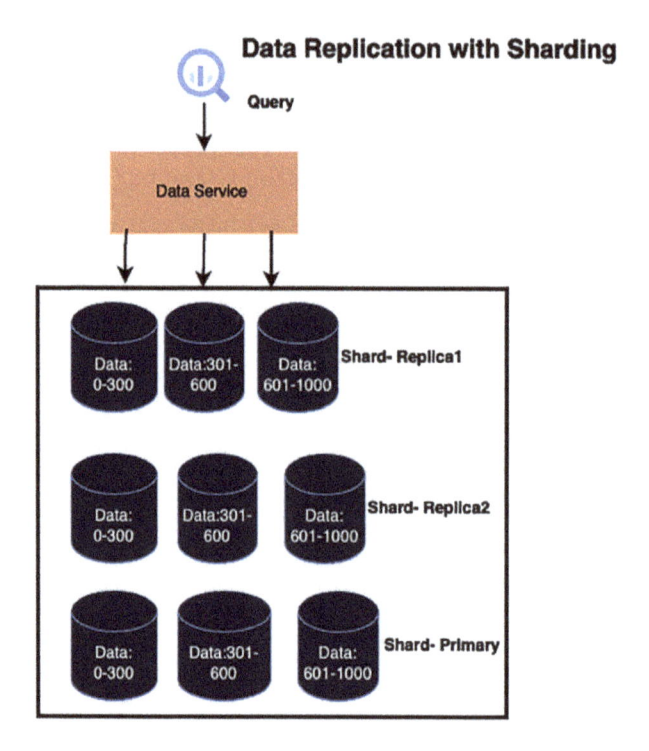

[Diagram showing a Query flowing into a Data Service, which distributes to three shards: Shard-Replica1, Shard-Replica2, and Shard-Primary. Each shard contains three data partitions: Data: 0-300, Data: 301-600, and Data: 601-1000.]

Parallel and Stream Processing: Parallel processing and stream processing enable security tools to handle large data volumes by processing multiple data streams simultaneously, allowing for real-time analysis and quicker threat detection. For instance, using Apache Spark for distributed processing of security logs across a cluster of nodes allows for rapid analysis of large datasets, while Apache Kafka streams real-time network traffic data for immediate processing, ensuring timely identification of security breaches.

Understanding Data Encryption

Data encryption is critical for safeguarding sensitive information across various states—whether in motion, in use, or at rest. It converts readable data into an unreadable format, accessible only through a decryption key. Encryption is essential in securing data, ensuring that it remains protected from unauthorized access, modification, or theft.

Types of Data Encryption:

Symmetric Encryption

Symmetric encryption relies on a single key for both encrypting and decrypting data, making it a fast and efficient method for securing large volumes of data. However, the effectiveness of this approach hinges on secure key management; if the key is compromised, the entire system's security is at risk. A common use case for symmetric encryption is the implementation of AES-256 in systems like Microsoft SQL Server's Transparent Data Encryption (TDE) or Amazon RDS, where it ensures that data at rest is automatically encrypted, providing a seamless and robust layer of security

Asymmetric Encryption

Asymmetric encryption uses a public key for encryption and a private key for decryption, making it ideal for securing communications and transactions. This method is commonly used in SSL/TLS certificates for HTTPS connections, ensuring that data exchanged between a web server and a client remains confidential. Tools like Let's Encrypt and AWS Certificate Manager automate the management of these certificates, providing a streamlined way to secure web applications and protect user data.

End-to-End Data Encryption Practices

Data in Use: Application-Level Encryption and Authentication

Protecting data during active processing requires robust application-level encryption and strong authentication mechanisms. For instance, in-memory data stores like Redis can be secured using Two-Way SSL (mutual SSL), where both the client and server authenticate each other to ensure that only trusted entities can access the data. This encryption is critical in environments where sensitive information is processed in real-time, such as session data in web applications. By integrating Redis with SSL/TLS, sensitive data remains protected even when it's being actively used by applications, ensuring both confidentiality and integrity.

Data in Transit: Secure Transmission with TLS/SSL

When data is in transit—moving across networks—encryption is essential to protect it from interception. Secure protocols like TLS/SSL ensure that data exchanges between clients and servers are encrypted, preventing unauthorized access. For example, when using Kafka to handle high-throughput, real-time data streams, implementing TLS encryption ensures that the data moving between Kafka brokers, clients, and ZooKeeper remains secure. This is particularly important in distributed systems where data travels across multiple network nodes, as it guards against man-in-the-middle attacks and ensures data integrity.

Data at Rest: Encryption with Robust Key Management

Encrypting data at rest is crucial for protecting stored information from unauthorized access, especially if the physical security of the storage medium is compromised. For example, in Elasticsearch, security configurations automatically generate TLS certificates and keys to secure the transport and HTTP layers. By using tools like AWS Key Management Service (KMS) or BitLocker, organizations can encrypt stored data, such as logs or customer records, ensuring that even if the storage device is accessed by unauthorized parties, the data remains unreadable without the decryption keys. Elasticsearch's automatic configuration of TLS for its data layers exemplifies how built-in security features can streamline the protection of data at rest in large-scale deployments.

By implementing comprehensive end-to-end encryption practices—securing data in use with application-level encryption and mutual authentication, encrypting data in transit with TLS/SSL, and safeguarding data at rest with strong encryption and key management—organizations can protect sensitive information throughout its lifecycle. These practices are essential in modern security tools, ensuring that data remains secure, private, and resilient against unauthorized access and cyber threats.

Major Compliance Requirements for Data Encryption

GDPR: Requires encryption to protect personal data within the EU.

HIPAA: Enforces encryption for sensitive health information.

PCI DSS: Mandates encryption of cardholder data during transmission and storage.

SOX: Requires encryption to protect financial data in public companies.

Data at the Core: Ensuring Availability, Localization, and Security

FISMA: Mandates encryption for federal information systems.

CCPA: Encourages encryption to protect consumer data in California.

Data encryption is essential for securing sensitive data, protecting against unauthorized access and breaches. By using both symmetric and asymmetric encryption and managing keys effectively, organizations can safeguard data at rest, in transit, and in use, ensuring a resilient security infrastructure that meets modern standards.

Data Localization: Why It Matters?

Data localization refers to the practice of storing and processing data within the geographic boundaries of the country where it is collected. This approach ensures that personal and sensitive information is governed by the local laws of the region, enhancing security and compliance. As global data flows increase, the need to protect data from unauthorized access, breaches, and foreign surveillance has become more pressing, making data localization a critical aspect of modern cybersecurity. Data localization is crucial for several reasons:

Legal Compliance: Many countries have enacted laws requiring that data related to their citizens be stored and processed within their borders. Regulations like the GDPR in Europe, India's Personal Data Protection Bill, and China's Cybersecurity Law are examples of such mandates.

Enhanced Security: Keeping data within national borders reduces the risk of unauthorized access by foreign entities and enhances protection against cyber threats.

National Sovereignty: Data localization supports national security by ensuring that critical information is subject to the legal framework of the country where it originates.

Improved Response Times: Storing data locally allows for faster response times to security incidents, as the data is closer to the point of use.

Conclusion

In this chapter, we explored the critical aspects of optimizing data availability, protection, and accessibility within security systems. As data breaches and cyber threats become increasingly prevalent, the importance of robust, scalable, and secure data pipelines is paramount. We emphasized the role of optimized data processing, including strategies like data sharding, in-memory processing, and asynchronous methods, to ensure that security systems are both responsive and resilient.

We also addressed the growing importance of data localization in response to stricter regulatory environments. Effective data localization requires a comprehensive understanding of legal requirements, strategic cloud infrastructure use, and robust security measures to keep sensitive data within controlled environments, thereby enhancing compliance and national security.

Finally, we examined the vital role of encryption in safeguarding data at rest, in transit, and in use. By implementing strong encryption protocols and effective key management, organizations can ensure that their data remains secure, even in the event of other security measures being compromised.

Key Takeaways

	Data Format Optimization	Improves query performance using efficient formats like Parquet
	In-Memory Processing	Reduces latency with fast data access using tools like Redis.
	Sharding and Replication	Enhances scalability and resilience with data distribution e.g. Kafka and Elasticsearch design.
	Symmetric Encryption	Uses a single key for fast, efficient encryption, ideal for large data volumes.
	Asymmetric Encryption	Utilizes a public-private key pair for secure communications, often used in SSL/TLS.
	End-to-End Encryption	Ensures data is encrypted during use, transit, and rest.
	Data in Use	Protects processing data with encryption and secure.
	Data in Transit	Secures data transfer with TLS/SSL protocols to prevent interception.
	Data at Rest	Encrypts stored data using tools like AWS KMS to prevent unauthorized access.

Beyond Firewalls: *Security at Scale*

| Data Localization | Keeps data within specific geographic boundaries to comply with local laws and enhance security. |
| Major Data Compliance (GDPR) | Ensures data protection and privacy for EU citizens, requiring strict data handling and encryption measures. |

Reference:

https://www.kiteworks.com/risk-compliance-glossary/data-localization/

https://blog.bytebytego.com/p/how-to-scale-a-website-to-support?utm_source=publication-search

https://medium.com/@mmoshikoo/cache-strategies-996e91c80303

https://www.yugabyte.com/blog/what-is-geo-distributed-application/

https://hazelcast.com/glossary/sharding/

https://www.manageengine.com/device-control/data-replication.html

https://www.imperva.com/learn/data-security/data-localization/

Data at the Core: Ensuring Availability, Localization, and Security

6

AI in Cybersecurity: Balancing Power and Vulnerabilities

As we've explored in previous chapters, advanced cybersecurity tools rely heavily on data collection and analysis to identify and mitigate threats. These tools increasingly leverage AI to enhance their capabilities, enabling faster, more accurate detection and response to complex cyber threats. However, as AI becomes more integral to cybersecurity, it also introduces new vulnerabilities. In this chapter, we will examine the dual-edged nature of AI in cybersecurity—its potential to strengthen security measures and the risks it poses if not properly managed.

We'll explore the vulnerabilities inherent in AI models, how they can be exploited, and the strategies to mitigate these risks. Additionally, we'll look at the compliance frameworks available to guide the ethical and secure development of AI in cybersecurity. Finally, we'll outline key considerations for designing and developing AI models that are robust, secure, and aligned with the latest industry standards. This chapter will equip we with the knowledge to leverage AI effectively while safeguarding against the unique challenges it brings to the cybersecurity landscape.

AI in Advanced Cybersecurity: Elevating Threat Detection

As cyber threats grow more sophisticated, integrating Artificial Intelligence (AI) into cybersecurity tools has become essential. Data analysis tools are proficient in analyzing data and detecting patterns, but AI takes these capabilities further by adding predictive intelligence and automation.

AI-Powered Data Processing and Automated Intelligence: Advanced tools excel at processing and analyzing data to uncover hidden patterns, but AI takes this a step further by using predictive models to forecast potential threats with greater precision. While data analysis identifies trends based on historical data, AI anticipates and counters threats before they even materialize.Moreover, AI introduces automation into cybersecurity, enabling real-time threat detection and response. Unlike traditional data analysis tools that require manual oversight, AI-driven systems can autonomously identify and neutralize threats, such as bot-driven assaults, without human intervention. This automated intelligence is critical for managing the complexity and speed of modern cyberattacks.

Strengthening Endpoint Protection and Behavioral Analysis: While advanced tools focus on pre-processing, analyzing, visualizing, and predicting data, AI takes this further by using predictive models to forecast future threats. Advanced tools rely on statistical methods to uncover patterns in data, whereas AI leverages complex algorithms to anticipate and counter potential risks.In endpoint protection, AI can continuously adapts to emerging threats, ensuring defenses remain strong as attack methods evolve. For behavioral analysis, AI can enhances fraud prevention by predicting and mitigating risks that might slip past conventional techniques.

AI-Enhanced Honeypots: Sophisticated Threat Detection: Honeypots are designed to attract attackers by emulating various services and systems, such as Windows or Linux servers, and a range of protocols like FTP, SSH, HTTP, HTTPS, and many more. The goal is to study attackers' methods and use that information to strengthen security controls. With the integration of AI, these honeypots become far more sophisticated. AI algorithms process the attack information in real time, generating data in a format that AI can analyze to detect and anticipate future attacks. This advanced processing capability allows the honeypot to adapt and respond more effectively, emulating any device or service while providing real-time alerts on detected threats. The result is a dynamic, AI-driven security tool that continuously learns from and defends against increasingly complex cyber threats.

AI integration elevates advanced cybersecurity tools, providing a proactive, intelligent approach to threat detection. By combining data analysis with AI's predictive power, organizations can build a more adaptive and resilient defense against the ever-evolving landscape of cyber threats.

Implementing AI for Advanced Security Tools:

Artificial Intelligence (AI) is transforming how we approach cybersecurity, especially in enhancing threat detection and risk analysis. By integrating AI into advanced security tools like behavior analysis and bot detection, organizations can proactively identify and mitigate threats. This guide outlines the steps to implement AI in our security framework, focusing on building machine learning models that enhance cybersecurity efforts.

Define the Security Objective: Start by clearly defining the security challenge we want to address with AI. Whether it's detecting unusual user behavior to prevent fraud, identifying malicious bots, or analyzing network traffic for potential threats, a well-defined objective will guide the entire AI implementation process.

Select the Right AI Model: Choose a machine learning model that fits our security objective. For behavior analysis, a model that can learn and predict user actions is essential. For bot detection, models that distinguish between human and automated behavior are key. The model choice depends on the complexity of the threats you're targeting and the type of data available.

Collect and Prepare Security Data: Gather relevant data that reflects the security scenarios we want to analyze. This might include user activity logs, network traffic records, or historical data on past security breaches. Data quality is crucial—clean and preprocess the data to ensure accuracy. In Chapter 5, we discussed how to enhance data management using techniques like sharding, replication, and data encryption to maintain data integrity and availability during analysis.

Train the Model: Train our AI model using the prepared data. During this phase, the model learns to recognize patterns indicative of security threats, such as abnormal user behavior or suspicious network traffic. Fine-tune the model by adjusting parameters to improve its accuracy in detecting threats. The goal is to build a model that can predict and respond to risks with high precision.

Evaluate and Validate the Model: Before deploying our AI-enhanced security tool, evaluate its performance using metrics like detection accuracy, false positive rates, and response time. Testing the model on the validation set will reveal its effectiveness in identifying threats. This step is crucial to ensure that the model reliably enhances our security posture without generating excessive false alerts.

Deploy and Continuously Monitor: Once validated, deploy our AI-powered security tool into our live environment. Continuous monitoring is essential to ensure the tool remains effective as new threats emerge. In Chapter 4, we emphasized the importance of observability and metrics for system performance, which also applies to monitoring AI models to ensure they stay relevant and effective.

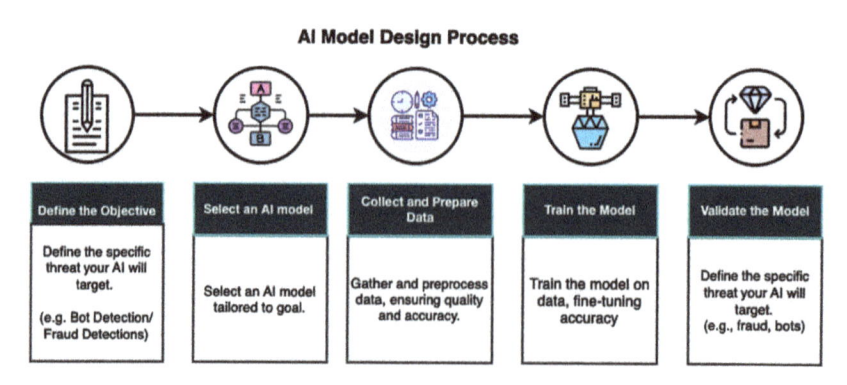

AI Model Design Process

Define the Objective	Select an AI model	Collect and Prepare Data	Train the Model	Validate the Model
Define the specific threat your AI will target. (e.g. Bot Detection/ Fraud Detections)	Select an AI model tailored to goal.	Gather and preprocess data, ensuring quality and accuracy.	Train the model on data, fine-tuning accuracy	Define the specific threat your AI will target. (e.g., fraud, bots)

This guide provides a focused approach to implementing AI in advanced security tools, emphasizing careful planning, data management, and ongoing evaluation. By following these steps, we can leverage AI to significantly enhance our organization's ability to detect and mitigate cybersecurity threats.

Challenges in Integrating AI into Cybersecurity

Incorporating AI into cybersecurity offers powerful advantages but also introduces new challenges. As AI enhances threat detection and automates defenses, it also faces vulnerabilities that can be exploited by rapidly evolving cyber threats. This section explores the key challenges of using AI in cybersecurity, laying the groundwork for understanding how to overcome these obstacles and build stronger, more resilient defenses.

Dynamic Cyber Tactics: Cybercriminals are highly adaptive, constantly developing new strategies and techniques to bypass security measures. AI systems, which are trained on existing data, often struggle to keep pace with these rapidly changing attack methods. As new types of threats emerge, AI models may fail to recognize them, leading to potential security breaches. This evolving nature of cyber threats creates a significant challenge for AI, as it requires continuous retraining and updates to remain effective.

Data Integrity and Poisoning Attacks: AI systems rely heavily on large datasets for training. However, if the data used for training is corrupted—whether intentionally through poisoning attacks or inadvertently—AI models can learn incorrect patterns. This can lead to vulnerabilities where the AI system misidentifies threats or, worse, becomes an enabler of attacks. Poisoning attacks are particularly insidious because they can be difficult to detect and can fundamentally undermine the AI's reliability.

Manipulation of AI Inputs: Adversarial attacks involve subtle modifications to input data that cause AI systems to make incorrect decisions. For example, by slightly altering the data fed into an AI model, attackers can trick the system into misclassifying malicious activities as benign. This type of attack poses a significant challenge because it exploits the very mechanisms that make AI effective—its ability to recognize patterns—by feeding it deceptive information.

Decreasing Model Accuracy Over Time: AI models are not static; they must be continually updated and retrained to maintain their accuracy. As the environment in which they operate changes, or as attackers develop new tactics, AI models can experience "model drift," where their effectiveness diminishes over time. This drift can lead to an increase in false positives and false negatives, reducing the overall reliability of the system.

Lack of Transparency and Explainability: Many AI systems, particularly those using deep learning, operate as "black boxes," where the decision-making process is not easily understood, even by experts. This lack of transparency can be a significant barrier to trust and adoption, especially in cybersecurity, where understanding the rationale behind decisions is crucial. It also complicates efforts to diagnose and fix issues when the AI system makes an error.

Bias and Ethical Concerns: AI systems can inherit biases from the data they are trained on. In cybersecurity, this can lead to disproportionate false positives or negatives for certain user groups, creating ethical and operational challenges. Bias in AI models can also lead to unfair outcomes, such as the misidentification of legitimate users as threats or the failure to recognize genuine threats in certain contexts.

Privacy and Data Protection Issues: AI systems in cybersecurity often process large amounts of sensitive data, which raises significant privacy concerns. Ensuring that this data is handled in compliance with regulations like GDPR and CCPA is crucial, yet challenging. The risk of data breaches or misuse of information by AI systems adds another layer of complexity to their deployment.

Inadequate AI Governance: The rapid adoption of AI in cybersecurity has outpaced the development of governance frameworks. Without clear standards and oversight, AI systems can be implemented in ways that are inconsistent or insecure, increasing the risk of errors and vulnerabilities. Establishing robust governance frameworks is essential to ensure that AI is used responsibly and effectively in cybersecurity.

These challenges underscore the complexity of integrating AI into cybersecurity and highlight the need for continuous adaptation, rigorous oversight, and careful consideration of the ethical implications. As we explore AI's role in cybersecurity further, it becomes clear that while AI offers powerful tools for defense, it also introduces new vulnerabilities that must be carefully managed.

Solutions for Integrating AI in Cybersecurity

As we navigate the complexities of implementing AI in cybersecurity, it is essential to focus on strategies that ensure AI enhances our security posture while mitigating potential risks. Here are key solutions for addressing the challenges associated with AI in threat detection:

Addressing Algorithmic Bias

- **Diverse Training Data:** Ensure our AI models are trained on datasets that reflect a wide range of demographics and scenarios to minimize bias. This diversity helps the AI make fair and accurate decisions across different contexts.

- **Continuous Monitoring and Auditing:** Regularly review and audit AI outputs to detect and correct biases. Implement feedback loops that allow for ongoing refinement and improvement of the AI models.

- **Ethical Frameworks:** Incorporate ethical guidelines into the AI development process, emphasizing fairness, transparency, and accountability in decision-making.

Optimizing Data Management

- **Data Governance and Localization:** Building on the concepts discussed in Chapter 5, it's crucial to implement robust data governance frameworks that ensure data quality, accessibility, and privacy. This involves setting clear standards for data collection, storage, and processing. By employing data localization strategies, sharding, and replication, organizations can optimize data availability and processing speed, ensuring that AI models have access to high-quality, localized data for more accurate predictions.

- **Data Diversity through Collaboration:** To enhance the robustness of AI models, collaborate with other organizations to access diverse datasets. This partnership approach ensures that AI models are trained on a wide range of data, which improves their relevance and effectiveness across different scenarios.

- **Data Preprocessing and Pipeline Optimization:** As we explored in Chapter 5, data preprocessing techniques such as cleaning, normalization, and the use of advanced data pipelines are essential. Implementing sharding and replication not only ensures data availability but also optimizes the speed and efficiency of AI model training, leading to more accurate and reliable outcomes.

Ensuring Data Privacy and Security

- **Advanced Cybersecurity Protocols:** Referencing our in-depth discussion in Chapter 5 on data encryption, it's imperative to implement strong cybersecurity protocols, including encryption and multi-factor authentication. These measures protect both AI systems and the data they process, ensuring that sensitive information is secure from unauthorized access and breaches.

- **Compliance and Ethical Accountability:** As outlined in earlier chapters, it's important to establish comprehensive frameworks that ensure AI systems operate within strict legal and ethical boundaries. This includes using advanced data encryption methods, sharding, and replication strategies to safeguard against data breaches, while also ensuring compliance with privacy regulations such as GDPR and HIPAA.

- **Continuous Monitoring and Auditing:** Building on the concepts of observability and metrics discussed in Chapter 4, organizations should implement continuous monitoring and regular audits of AI systems. This proactive approach helps identify and address vulnerabilities, ensuring that AI models remain compliant with privacy standards and are resilient against emerging threats.

Building AI Expertise:

- **Partnerships with Educational Institutions:** Collaborate with universities and training platforms to cultivate a pipeline of skilled AI professionals.

- **Employee Training Programs:** Invest in upskilling our workforce with AI knowledge, creating a strong internal talent pool capable of managing and advancing AI initiatives.

Cost-Effective AI Implementation:

- **Leverage Open-Source Tools:** Utilize open-source AI platforms and algorithms to reduce costs while maintaining flexibility in development.

- **Off-the-Shelf Solutions:** Consider pre-built AI solutions that can be tailored to our needs, offering a balance between customization and cost efficiency.

- **Training and In-House Development:** Invest in training programs to build an in-house AI team, reducing long-term reliance on external vendors.

Transparency and Interpretability in AI:

- **Explainable AI (XAI):** Adopt AI models that are transparent and interpretable, such as decision trees, to provide clear reasoning behind AI decisions.

- **Diverse AI Development Teams:** Ensure our AI teams include experts from various fields, including ethics and law, to enhance transparency and accountability.

- **User Education:** Educate stakeholders on how AI systems work, highlighting their strengths and limitations to build trust and understanding.

By strategically implementing these solutions, organizations can harness the full potential of AI in cybersecurity, ensuring robust protection while navigating the challenges inherent in AI deployment. The key lies in balancing innovation with caution, integrating AI seamlessly into existing security frameworks, and continuously refining AI models to stay ahead of emerging threats.

Available AI Governance Frameworks

The rapid advancement of AI technologies demands a robust governance framework to manage risks and ensure responsible use. AI governance is crucial for several reasons: it safeguards ethics and human rights by preventing AI from infringing on privacy or enabling discrimination; it ensures transparency and accountability, building trust in AI systems by making decisions traceable; it facilitates effective risk management, addressing both technical failures and ethical issues like bias; and it enhances safety and security, protecting AI systems from cyber threats and preventing harmful outcomes.As AI continues to evolve, several frameworks have emerged to guide its responsible development and deployment:

NIST AI RMF: The National Institute of Standards and Technology's AI Risk Management Framework focuses on identifying and managing risks associated with AI systems. It provides organizations with tools and practices to ensure that AI technologies are trustworthy and reliable.

EU AI Act: The European Union's AI Act is a legal framework aimed at regulating high-risk AI systems. It sets out requirements for transparency, accountability, and safety, ensuring that AI systems deployed in critical areas meet stringent standards.

OECD AI Principles: The Organization for Economic Co-operation and Development (OECD) has established guidelines for trustworthy AI, emphasizing principles such as fairness, transparency, and accountability.

ISO/IEC 42001: This international standard provides a framework for AI governance, ensuring that AI systems are developed and managed in a way that is consistent with global best practices.

Challenges with AI Governance

Despite the existence of these frameworks, governing AI presents significant challenges:

Complexity and the "Black Box" Nature of AI: Many AI models, especially those based on deep learning, are often described as "black boxes" because their internal workings are not easily understood, even by their creators. This lack of transparency makes it difficult to ensure that AI systems operate in line with ethical standards and regulatory requirements.

Bias in AI Systems: AI systems can inadvertently perpetuate biases present in their training data, leading to unfair or discriminatory outcomes. Addressing this issue requires continuous monitoring and updating of AI models to ensure they do not reinforce harmful biases.

Global Nature of AI Development: AI systems are often developed, trained, and deployed across multiple countries, each with its own regulations and standards. This global nature makes it challenging to enforce consistent governance and can lead to gaps in oversight and potential vulnerabilities.

Conclusion:

Integrating AI into advanced security tools, such as behavior analysis and bot detection, significantly enhances threat detection and risk analysis by enabling systems to learn from data, predict threats, and respond with precision. Proper AI implementation requires careful planning, from defining the security challenge to training and refining the model, ensuring robust AI-driven security solutions that effectively counter evolving cyber threats.

As AI becomes more pervasive, the need for comprehensive governance and regulation grows. Understanding AI's capabilities and associated risks is essential to ensuring its safe and ethical use. By adopting and adapting existing frameworks and addressing AI governance challenges, we can harness AI's transformative power while safeguarding against potential dangers.

Reference

https://owasp.org/www-project-top-10-for-large-language-model-applications/assets/PDF/OWASP-Top-10-for-LLMs-2023-v1_1.pdf

https://www.ibm.com/topics/generative-ai

https://secureframe.com/blog/how-will-ai-affect-cybersecurity

https://kpmg.com/ch/en/insights/cybersecurity-risk/artificial-intelligence-influences.html

https://www.gptechblog.com/what-is-generative-ai-comprehensive-guide-beginners/

7

A Step-by-Step Guide to Building a Robust Security Framework

As cyber threats continue to evolve in complexity and frequency, the need for a robust and adaptive security framework has never been more critical. This chapter is designed to guide we through the essential steps required to develop a comprehensive security strategy that integrates traditional tools, advanced technologies, and AI-driven solutions. Whether we are looking to strengthen existing defenses or build a new security system from the ground up, this chapter provides a clear, step-by-step guide to ensure our organization is well-protected against modern threats.

The following sections will not only offer detailed instructions but will also serve as a practical checklist. This will help we verify that our security measures are comprehensive, up-to-date, and capable of responding to the ever-changing landscape of cyber threats. By following this guide, we can ensure that our organization is equipped with the right tools and strategies to defend against potential risks, maintain compliance, and protect critical assets.

Step 1: Network Security - Foundation of a Secure Environment

Network Security will cover essential aspects of securing our organization's network, including segmentation to minimize risks, configuring firewalls for controlled access, deploying intrusion detection and prevention systems to monitor for threats, ensuring secure remote access with VPNs, and enforcing network access control to allow only compliant devices. This comprehensive approach helps establish a strong, layered defense to safeguard our digital assets.

Network Segmentation

- **Segment the Network:** Break down the network into smaller, isolated segments (e.g., by department or function) to minimize the attack surface.

- **Use VLANs:** Implement VLANs (Virtual LANs) to logically separate different network segments, reducing the risk of lateral movement by attackers.

- **Micro-segmentation:** Consider implementing micro-segmentation within VLANs for even more granular control, particularly for sensitive or high-risk areas of the network.

- **Firewalls Between Segments:** Deploy firewalls like Palo Alto Networks or Cisco ASA to enforce security policies between these segments.

Firewall Configuration

- **Deploy Firewalls:** Place firewalls at the network perimeter and between segments. Configure them to allow only necessary traffic while blocking unauthorized access.

- **Regular Rule Review:** Regularly review and update firewall rules to address emerging threats. Remove outdated or unused rules to reduce complexity and potential vulnerabilities.

- **Advanced Threat Protection:** Consider using next-generation firewalls (NGFW) that include advanced threat protection features, such as deep packet inspection (DPI) and sandboxing.

Intrusion Detection and Prevention

- **IDS/IPS Deployment:** Implement IDS/IPS (Intrusion Detection/Prevention Systems) like Snort or Suricata to monitor network traffic for malicious activity.

- **Integration with SIEM:** Integrate IDS/IPS with SIEM (Security Information and Event Management) systems like Splunk to correlate events and detect potential breaches in real-time.

- **Behavioral Analysis:** Incorporate AI-driven behavioral analysis tools to detect anomalies that traditional IDS/IPS might miss.

Virtual Private Network (VPN)

- **Deploy VPN Solutions:** Use VPN solutions like OpenVPN or Cisco AnyConnect to secure remote access to the network. Ensure all remote connections are encrypted and authenticated.

- **Multi-Factor Authentication (MFA):** Implement MFA for VPN access to add an additional layer of security, ensuring that only authorized users can access the network remotely.

- **Monitor VPN Usage:** Regularly monitor and log VPN connections to detect any unusual or unauthorized access attempts.

Network Access Control (NAC)

- **Enforce NAC Policies:** Use NAC solutions to enforce security policies at the point of entry. Ensure that only devices meeting security standards can connect to the network.
- **Device Profiling:** Profile and categorize devices connecting to the network, applying appropriate security policies based on the device type, user role, and risk level.
- **Continuous Monitoring:** Continuously monitor devices on the network for compliance with security policies, and take action if a device becomes non-compliant.

Network Traffic Encryption

- **Encrypt Data in Transit:** Ensure that sensitive data transmitted across the network is encrypted using protocols like TLS or IPsec.
- **Certificate Management:** Regularly update and manage digital certificates to prevent unauthorized access and ensure secure communication channels.

Zero Trust Network Access (ZTNA)

- **Implement Zero Trust Principles:** Adopt a Zero Trust approach, where no user or device is trusted by default, even if they are within the network perimeter. Continuously verify and monitor access based on user identity, device health, and the context of the request.

- **Least Privilege Access:** Ensure that users and devices have the minimum necessary access to perform their tasks, reducing the potential impact of a security breach.

Regular Audits and Penetration Testing

- **Conduct Network Audits:** Regularly audit network security configurations, policies, and devices to ensure they align with current security standards and best practices.

- **Penetration Testing:** Perform regular penetration testing to identify and address vulnerabilities within the network infrastructure before attackers can exploit them.

Step 2: Application Security - Building Secure Software

Application security is vital in safeguarding software from vulnerabilities that can be exploited by malicious actors. To ensure a secure application environment, it's essential to integrate security measures throughout the entire software development lifecycle (SDLC), from design to deployment and beyond.

Adopt Secure Coding Practices

- **Developer Training:** Ensure that developers are well-versed in secure coding practices, emphasizing the importance of avoiding common vulnerabilities such as SQL injection, Cross-Site Scripting (XSS), and buffer overflows.

- **Code Review:** Implement regular peer code reviews focusing on security aspects. This step allows developers to identify potential security flaws early in the development process.

- **Code Analysis Tools:** Utilize static code analysis tools like SonarQube, Veracode, or Checkmarx to automatically scan code for vulnerabilities. These tools help detect issues like insecure data handling and improper error handling before the code is deployed.

Implement Comprehensive Security Testing

- **Automated Testing:** Use automated security testing tools like OWASP ZAP or Burp Suite to continuously test our applications for vulnerabilities. These tools simulate attacks to uncover weaknesses that could be exploited.

- **Penetration Testing:** Conduct regular penetration tests to identify and address vulnerabilities that automated tools might miss. Penetration testing involves ethical hacking techniques to simulate real-world attack scenarios.

- **DAST and SAST Tools:** Incorporate both Dynamic Application Security Testing (DAST) and Static Application Security Testing (SAST) to test applications at various stages of development. DAST tools test running applications for security vulnerabilities, while SAST tools analyze the source code or binary code for security flaws.

- **Interactive Application Security Testing (IAST):** Implement IAST solutions to continuously monitor applications during runtime, providing real-time feedback on vulnerabilities as they occur.

Manage Dependencies and Third-Party Components

- **Regular Updates:** Keep all third-party libraries and dependencies up to date to patch known vulnerabilities. This is crucial since many attacks exploit outdated components with known security flaws.

- **Dependency Scanning:** Use tools like Dependabot, Snyk, or WhiteSource to automate the scanning of dependencies and ensure they are free of vulnerabilities. These tools alert we when a dependency needs updating or has a known security issue.

- **Software Composition Analysis (SCA):** Incorporate SCA tools to analyze the security of open-source components and third-party libraries used within our application. SCA tools can identify licensing issues and vulnerabilities in the software supply chain.

Integrate Security into DevSecOps (Development, Security, and Operations)

- **CI/CD Integration:** Embed security checks into our Continuous Integration/Continuous Deployment (CI/CD) pipelines. Use tools like Jenkins, GitLab CI, or Azure DevOps to automate security testing as part of the build and deployment process.

- **Automated Security Gates:** Implement security gates within our DevOps pipelines that prevent deployment if critical vulnerabilities are detected. This ensures that only secure code is promoted to production.

- **Container Security:** For applications deployed in containers, use tools like Docker Bench Security, Anchore, or Aqua Security to scan container images for vulnerabilities and ensure that they adhere to security best practices.

- **Infrastructure as Code (IaC) Security:** Secure our infrastructure by using IaC security tools like Terraform, AWS CloudFormation, and HashiCorp Vault. These tools help manage and automate secure infrastructure configurations, reducing the risk of misconfigurations that could lead to security breaches.

Implement Secure Software Design

- **Threat Modeling:** Conduct threat modeling sessions during the design phase to identify potential security threats and vulnerabilities. This proactive approach helps in designing security controls to mitigate identified risks.

- **Secure Architecture Patterns:** Follow secure software architecture patterns, such as the principle of least privilege, defense in depth, and secure data flow, to build resilient applications.

- **Security Requirements:** Define and document security requirements as part of the project's functional and non-functional requirements. Ensure that these requirements are aligned with industry standards like OWASP, NIST, or ISO 27001.

Monitor and Respond to Security Incidents

- **Application Logging and Monitoring:** Implement robust logging and monitoring solutions to track application activity and detect anomalies in real-time. Use tools like ELK Stack, Splunk, or Prometheus to collect and analyze logs for signs of security breaches.

- **Incident Response Plan:** Develop and maintain an incident response plan specific to application security. This plan should outline the steps to take in the event of a security breach, including communication protocols, containment strategies, and recovery procedures.

- **Security Patching:** Establish a process for quickly applying security patches to applications and underlying infrastructure. Regularly review and update our patch management practices to ensure that vulnerabilities are addressed promptly.

Implement Strong Access Controls

- **Role-Based Access Control (RBAC):** Apply RBAC principles to ensure that users have the minimum level of access required to perform their duties. This limits the potential impact of compromised accounts.

- **Multi-Factor Authentication (MFA):** Enforce MFA for accessing sensitive application components, particularly for administrative accounts and users with elevated privileges.

- **Session Management:** Implement secure session management practices, such as setting appropriate session timeouts, using secure cookies, and preventing session fixation attacks.

Ensure Data Security

- **Data Encryption:** Encrypt sensitive data at rest and in transit using strong encryption algorithms. As discussed in Chapter 5, data encryption helps protect against data breaches and unauthorized access.

- **Data Privacy Compliance:** Ensure that our application complies with data privacy regulations like GDPR, CCPA, or HIPAA. Implement features like data anonymization, consent management, and user data access controls to meet regulatory requirements.

- **Data Integrity:** Implement measures to ensure data integrity, such as checksums, hashing, and digital signatures, to protect data from tampering or corruption.

By following these comprehensive best practices, organizations can significantly enhance the security of their applications, reducing the risk of breaches and ensuring that security is an integral part of the software development process.

Step 3: Information Security - Safeguarding Data Integrity

Information security is critical in protecting sensitive data from unauthorized access, alteration, and destruction. A strong information security strategy is essential to maintain data integrity and ensure that your organization's data is secure at all times.

Data Encryption

- **Protect Data at Rest and in Transit:** Encrypt sensitive data both when it is stored and when it is being transmitted. Utilize tools like AWS Key Management Service (KMS) or HashiCorp Vault for managing encryption keys and automating the rotation of certificates.

Access Controls

- **Role-Based Access Control (RBAC):** Implement RBAC to ensure that users only have access to the data necessary for their roles. Tools like Okta or Microsoft Azure Active Directory (AD) can help enforce these policies.

- **Multi-Factor Authentication (MFA):** Add an extra layer of security by enabling MFA for all users, particularly for those accessing sensitive information.

Backup and Disaster Recovery

- **Robust Backup Strategy:** Use reliable backup solutions like Veeam or AWS Backup to create secure, encrypted backups of critical data. Ensure these backups are stored securely off-site.

- **Disaster Recovery Planning:** Develop and maintain a comprehensive disaster recovery plan. Regularly test this plan to ensure that data can be quickly restored in the event of an incident.

Data Loss Prevention (DLP)

- **Monitor and Protect Sensitive Data:** Implement DLP solutions such as Symantec DLP or Microsoft 365 DLP to monitor and prevent the unauthorized movement or exfiltration of sensitive data.

By following these steps, you can create a robust information security framework that protects the integrity, confidentiality, and availability of your organization's critical data.

Step 4: Operational Security - Maintaining a Secure Operating Environment

Operational security focuses on securing your organization's daily operations by implementing controls and processes that protect critical assets and ensure continuity in the face of threats.

Change Management

- **Control and Document Changes:** Implement rigorous change management processes to oversee and document all system and application changes. Tools like ServiceNow can help track changes, ensuring compliance and reducing the risk of unauthorized modifications.

Device Access Control

- **Restrict Access to Critical Devices:** Limit both physical and remote access to essential devices. Use Network Access Control (NAC) solutions to enforce security policies for all connected devices, ensuring only authorized users and devices can access critical systems.

Least Privilege Access

- **Enforce Minimal Access Rights:** Implement a least privilege access policy across all systems, ensuring users have only the permissions necessary for their roles. Regularly audit access controls and adjust permissions to minimize risk.

Incident Response Plan

- **Prepare and Test Response Procedures:** Develop a comprehensive incident response plan, clearly defining communication protocols, roles, and procedures for various types of incidents. Regularly test the plan to ensure your team is prepared to respond swiftly and effectively.

Automation and Monitoring:

- **Automate and Continuously Monitor:** Utilize Security Orchestration, Automation, and Response (SOAR) platforms to automate security tasks, reducing human error. Implement continuous monitoring of systems and networks to detect and respond to anomalies early, ensuring a proactive security posture.

These steps will help maintain a secure operating environment, ensuring your organization is resilient against potential threats and prepared to respond effectively to any security incidents.

Step 5: Advanced Security Tools - Enhancing Protection

Incorporating advanced cybersecurity tools into your security strategy is crucial for addressing sophisticated threats and safeguarding critical assets. These tools provide additional layers of defense, enabling a more resilient and proactive security posture. Below are the steps to effectively introduce and integrate these advanced tools into your security operations.

Bot Detection and Fraud Prevention

- **Data Collection and Modeling:** Begin by collecting relevant data on user behavior, transaction patterns, and network traffic. Use this data to build machine learning models that can identify patterns indicative of bot activity or fraudulent behavior. Technologies like bot management systems can help automate the data collection and analysis process.

- **Scoring and Blocking:** Implement a scoring system that assesses each request or transaction based on the likelihood of it being malicious. Requests that exceed a certain risk threshold can be automatically blocked or flagged for further investigation. AI-driven fraud prevention tools can be integrated to enhance this process.

- **Continuous Improvement:** Regularly update your models and scoring criteria based on new threat intelligence and observed attack patterns. This ensures that your bot detection and fraud prevention systems remain effective against evolving threats.

Endpoint Protection

- **Telemetry and Behavioral Analysis:** Integrate JavaScript-based telemetry into your applications to monitor user interactions and detect abnormal behavior. This telemetry data can feed into Endpoint Detection and Response (EDR) systems to identify potential threats in real-time.

- **Automated Threat Response:** Configure your EDR tools to automatically respond to detected threats by isolating compromised endpoints, terminating malicious processes, or rolling back unauthorized changes. Endpoint protection technologies provide robust protection and real-time response capabilities.

- **Ongoing Monitoring:** Continuously monitor endpoint activity for signs of compromise. Use machine learning models to analyze telemetry data and detect deviations from normal behavior that could indicate an attack.

Threat Intelligence

- **Integration with Existing Tools:** Incorporate threat intelligence feeds into your existing security tools like SIEM, IDS/IPS, and firewalls. Use threat intelligence platforms to gather and analyze threat data, which can then be used to update your security policies and rules in real-time.

- **Signal Gathering:** Gather signals from various sources, including IP clean lists, ASN (Autonomous System Number) records, and domain reputation databases. This data helps in identifying malicious actors and allows for more precise threat detection and response.

- **Automated Threat Scoring:** Develop a threat scoring system based on the intelligence received. This system can help prioritize threats and automate responses to high-risk incidents. For example, if a new vulnerability is detected in the wild, your IDS/IPS can be updated automatically to protect against it.

- **Continuous Threat Analysis:** Regularly update your threat intelligence models and scoring systems to reflect the latest threat landscape. Automate the integration of new threat intelligence into your security infrastructure to maintain up-to-date defenses.

Deception Technology

- **Deploy Honeypots and Decoys:** Set up deception technologies like honeypots and decoy systems across your network. Use AI to monitor interactions with these decoys in real-time, providing early detection of sophisticated attackers.

- **Data Collection and Analysis:** Gather data on attacker behavior from interactions with the decoys. Use this data to refine your threat detection models and improve your overall security posture. Deception technologies can help automate this process.

- **Integrate with Security Infrastructure:** Ensure that your deception technology is integrated with other security tools, such as SIEM and EDR systems. This integration allows for seamless detection, analysis, and response to threats detected through the decoys.

By following these steps, you can effectively introduce and integrate advanced security tools into your existing cybersecurity framework. This comprehensive approach ensures that your organization is equipped to handle sophisticated threats, providing a robust and proactive defense against potential cyberattacks.

Step 6: Implementing AI in Security: A Step-by-Step Approach

Start small by targeting one specific threat to enhance using AI. Begin by defining the security challenge, such as detecting fraudulent behavior or identifying bot traffic.

- **Select and Train the AI Model:** Choose a suitable AI model based on your target threat. Train it using relevant, high-quality data that reflects real security scenarios.

- **Evaluate the Model:** Test the AI model to ensure it accurately detects the threat. Adjust and fine-tune the model based on the results to improve its performance.

- **Deploy and Monitor:** Implement the AI model in your security environment. Continuously monitor its effectiveness and make adjustments as needed to adapt to new threats.

- **Scale Gradually:** After successful implementation, move on to the next security threat. Repeat the process, ensuring each AI model is regularly reviewed and fine-tuned for optimal performance.

By taking these manageable steps, you can incrementally enhance your security posture with AI, ensuring a robust defense against evolving cyber threats.

Conclusion

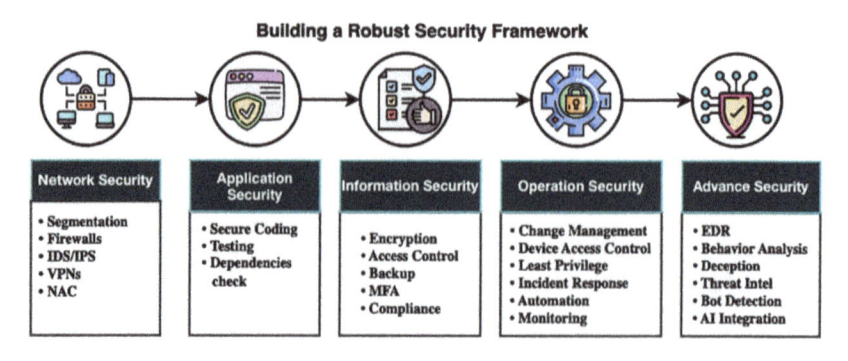

Building a Robust Security Framework

Network Security	Application Security	Information Security	Operation Security	Advance Security
• Segmentation • Firewalls • IDS/IPS • VPNs • NAC	• Secure Coding • Testing • Dependencies check	• Encryption • Access Control • Backup • MFA • Compliance	• Change Management • Device Access Control • Least Privilege • Incident Response • Automation • Monitoring	• EDR • Behavior Analysis • Deception • Threat Intel • Bot Detection • AI Integration

In conclusion, traditional cybersecurity methods form the essential foundation of any robust security strategy. These time-tested practices—such as network segmentation, firewall configuration, and access control—are indispensable for establishing a secure environment. However, as cyber threats become more sophisticated, the integration of advanced tools becomes increasingly important. Technologies like behavioral analysis, deception tactics, and threat intelligence significantly enhance our ability to detect, respond to, and prevent complex attacks.

The introduction of AI into the cybersecurity landscape offers even greater potential for modernization. When implemented correctly, AI can revolutionize security operations by automating threat detection, analyzing vast amounts of data in real-time, and predicting potential risks before they materialize. By combining the solid core of traditional cybersecurity with the cutting-edge capabilities of advanced tools and AI, organizations can create a dynamic, adaptive security framework that is well-equipped to handle the evolving challenges of the digital age.

Reference

https://synoptek.com/insights/it-blogs/reduce-cost-implementing-effective-cybersecurity-plan/

https://purplesec.us/learn/cyber-security-strategy/

https://www.netgainit.com/blogs/cyber-security-implementation-plan/

https://gcore.com/learning/cybersecurity-solutions-overview/

https://www.institutedata.com/us/blog/implementing-cybersecurity-models/#:~:text=Steps%20to%20implement%20a%20cybersecurity%20model&text=This%20involves%20identifying%20and%20understanding,risk's%20likelihood%20and%20potential%20impact.

https://hbr.org/2023/05/cybersecurity-needs-to-be-part-of-our-products-design-from-the-start

https://sre.google/sre-book/table-of-contents/

Beyond Firewalls: *Security at Scale*

Printed in the USA
CPSIA information can be obtained
at www.ICGtesting.com
CBHW040947181124
17427CB00067B/854